Pagan Portals

Sumer Is Icumen In

How-To Survive (and Enjoy) the
Mid-Summer Festival

Pagan Portals

Sumer Is Icumen In

How-To Survive (and Enjoy) the
Mid-Summer Festival

Mélusine Draco

MOON
BOOKS
Winchester, UK
Washington, USA

JOHN HUNT PUBLISHING

First published by Moon Books, 2022
Moon Books is an imprint of John Hunt Publishing Ltd., No. 3 East Street, Alresford
Hampshire SO24 9EE, UK
office@jhpbooks.net
www.johnhuntpublishing.com
www.moon-books.net

For distributor details and how to order please visit the 'Ordering' section on our website.

Design: Matthew Greenfield

UK: Printed and bound by CPI Group (UK) Ltd, Croydon, CR0 4YY
Printed in North America by CPI GPS partners

We operate a distinctive and ethical publishing philosophy in
all areas of our business, from our global network of authors to
production and worldwide distribution.

Contents

Sumer Is Icumen In
How-To Survive (and Enjoy) the Mid-Summer Festival

Is a companion volume to...

Have a cool Yule
How-To Survive (and Enjoy) the Mid-Winter Festival

978-1-78535-711-4 (Paperback)
978-1-78535-712-1 (e-book)

Chapter One

Sumer Is Icumen In

Although the title of *Sumer Is Icumen In* (also called *Summer Cannon* or *Cuckoo Song*) may not look like modern English, it is considered the oldest existing English song, dating back to medieval England in the mid-13th century and written in the Wessex dialect of Middle English. And, although towards the middle of the year the internet is full of pagan postings referring to the Mid-Summer Festival, most of them demonstrate a sad lack of awareness concerning our indigenous pagan ancestry and its customs. Let's understand one thing before we go further: the Church did *not* invent the Mid-Summer Festival ... it was there with all its rich panoply of feasting and celebration long before it entered the church calendar as Saint John's Day.

The feast day of John the Baptist, wasn't established by the Church until the 4th century AD to honour of the birth of the saint, which the Bible records as being six-months before that of Jesus. Conveniently, this coincided with the major celebration of the old Mid-Summer Festival, or Summer Solstice on or around the 21st June which allowed it to correspond with the official birth day of Jesus that would henceforth be celebrated on the 25th December – the Winter Solstice (and the official birthday of the military deity, Mithras, so popular with the Roman legions).

In the Old Ways, the Summer Solstice marks the mid-point of the growing season, halfway between planting and harvest. It is traditionally known as one of four 'quarter days' in some cultures that folk celebrated by feasting, dancing, singing, and preparing for the hot summer days ahead. 24th June remains a quarter day in England, Wales, and Ireland, although the celebration *predates* Christianity, and existed under different names and traditions around the world, latterly being commemorated by many

Christian denominations, such as the Roman Catholic Church, Lutheran Churches, and Anglican Communion, as well as by Freemasonry. The observance begins the evening before, now referred to as St John's Eve, starting at sunset on 23rd June, the eve of celebration before the Feast Day of the saint – whereas we in traditional British Old Craft retain the 21st June as the focus of our devotions.

Or, as it is known in many parts of Ireland, Bonfire Night, which was traditionally marked by the construction of large fires throughout the countryside. These were lit at sundown and were the focal point of popular communal festivities. People gathered to dance and sing, while young men proved their bravery by leaping through the flames. The night was also rich in folklore, much of it concerned with fertility! Prayers and rhymes were recited to ensure a plentiful harvest and, indeed, the fire itself was thought to have magical powers. Burning weeds in its flames would prevent arable fields from becoming overgrown, while scattering its ashes would guarantee the land's fertility. Similarly parading through the fields with lighted branches from the bonfire would protect the crops from disease and pestilence. It was also deemed particularly lucky to bring the ashes home to rekindle on the kitchen hearth. Although most of these customs are no longer practiced, lighting St. John's bonfires still takes places in many parts of Ireland (especially the west). It is hardly a coincidence that these fires are lit so close to the Summer Solstice, which points to this custom having its roots in the Elder Faith.

The Summer Solstice is the longest day in the northern hemisphere and either falls on the 20th or 21st of June, whilst Midsummer's Day in Europe is traditionally on 24 June; a discrepancy caused by the variants of the Julian Calendar, misappropriation by the Church and further confused by the introduction of the Gregorian Calendar. Traditionally, Midsummer's Eve is a time associated with witches, magic, fairies and dancing with bonfires lit all over the country. This was in praise of the sun, for as from today, the days would begin getting shorter and the sun gradually appeared to be getting weaker, so people would light fires to try and strengthen the sun. Practice of this ancient ritual, which also includes a Summer Solstice Circle Dance, is now mainly confined to Cornwall and the West Country.

During the Summer Solstice, the earth's axis is tilted at its closest point from the sun. This means that in the northern hemisphere, the sun is at its highest point in the sky. It's also the longest day of the year – and the shortest night. It would have been relatively easy for prehistoric people to observe the rising and setting positions of the sun each day, and to mark these orientations from any given spot. The longest day of the year would have perhaps been a time of celebration, with warm nights and long daylight making it the perfect time to gather together for an in-gathering.

The Summer Solstice has been celebrated by many different cultures and societies across the world. Elsewhere in the British Isles, Neolithic passage tombs such as *Bryn Celli Ddu* on Anglesey in North Wales and Townleyhall in Co. Louth, Ireland, are also aligned with the midsummer sunrise, when the sun shines down the passage into the inner chambers. The tallest stone of the circle at Castlerigg marks the north-west midsummer sunset. At Fajada Butte, a Native American site in New Mexico, USA, a shaft of sunlight through a gap between two slabs of rock bisects a spiral carving around noon on the Summer Solstice. While in 16th century China, the emperor conducted ceremonies at midsummer solstice at the Temple of the Earth, presenting offerings to the sky and the gods. In Northern Europe, midsummer was celebrated from pre-Christian times until the mid-19th century, with festivals during which bonfires were the focal point of the gathering.

A 13th-century monk of Winchcomb, Gloucestershire, who

compiled a book of sermons for Christian feast days, recorded how St. John's Eve was celebrated in his time, although these customs were probably throw-backs to older Midsummer rites:

> Let us speak of the revels which are accustomed to be made on St. John's Eve, of which there are three kinds. On St. John's Eve in certain regions the boys collect bones and certain other rubbish, and burn them, and therefrom a smoke is produced on the air. They also make brands and go about the fields with the brands. Thirdly, the wheel which they roll. Saint John's Fires, explained the monk of Winchcombe, were to drive away dragons, which were abroad on St. John's Eve, poisoning springs and wells. The wheel that was rolled downhill he gave its explanation: 'The wheel is rolled to signify that the sun then rises to the highest point of its circle and at once turns back; thence it comes that the wheel is rolled.

On St John's Day c.1333, Petrarch watched the women of Cologne rinsing their hands and arms in the Rhine 'so that the threatening calamities of the coming year might be washed away by bathing in the river'. The15th-century diarist, Goro Dati, described the celebration of Saint John's Day at Midsummer in Italy as being 'one in which guilds prepared their workshops with fine displays, and one in which solemn church processions took place, with men dressed in the costumes of Christian saints and angels.'

In the 16th century, the historian John Stow, described the celebration of Midsummer:

> The wealthier sort also before their doors near to the said bonfires would set out tables on the vigils furnished with sweet bread and good drink, and on the festival days with meats and drinks plentifully, whereunto they would invite their neighbours and passengers also to sit, and to be merry with them in great familiarity, praising God

for his benefits bestowed on them. These were called bonfires as well of good amity amongst neighbours that, being before at controversy, were there by the labour of others reconciled, and made of bitter enemies, loving friends, as also for the virtue that a great fire to purge the infection of the air. On the vigil of St John Baptist and St Peter and Paul the Apostles, every man's door being shadowed with green birch, long fennel, St John's Wort, Orpin, white lillies and such like, garnished upon with garlands of beautiful flowers, had also lamps of glass, with oil burning in them all night, some hung branches of iron curiously wrought, containing hundreds of lamps lit at once, which made goodly show.

These fires are commonly called 'Saint John's Fires' in various languages, such as the 'lighting of festive fires upon St. John's Eve is first recorded as a popular custom by Jean Belethus, a theologian at the University of Paris, in the early twelfth century'. In England, the earliest reference to this custom occurs in the 13th century AD, in the *Liber Memorandum* of the parish church at Barnwell in the Nene Valley, which stated that parish youth would gather on the day to sing songs and play games, and served to repel witches and evil spirits. Saint John's Day was also a popular day for infant baptisms and in the 19th century, 'baptisms of children who had died 'pagans' were acted out'. In Sweden, young people visited holy springs as 'a reminder of how Saint John baptised Christ in the River Jordan. In addition, historically, 'it was a custom to carry lighted torches on Midsummer Eve, as an emblem of St. John the Baptist, who was 'a burning and shining light, and the preparer of the way of Christ'.

In common with their usual assimilations of pagan festivals, no doubt the Church adapted yet another pre-Christian festival celebrating the Summer Solstice as a Christian holiday by moving back a couple of days. The Midsummer Festival, now with Saint John's Day-related traditions, church services, and celebrations became particularly important in northern Europe – Sweden, Denmark, Norway, Finland, Estonia, Latvia and Lithuania – and very strongly observed in Poland, Russia, Belarus, Germany, Netherlands, Flanders, Ireland, parts of the United Kingdom (Cornwall especially), France, Italy, Malta, Portugal, Spain, Ukraine, other parts of Europe, and elsewhere – such as Canada, the United States, Puerto Rico, and also in the Southern Hemisphere (mostly in Brazil, Argentina and Australia). In Estonia, Latvia, Lithuania and Quebec (Canada), the traditional Midsummer Day was a public holiday. As it was in Sweden and Finland, but in the 1950s, it was moved to the Friday and Saturday between June 19 and June 26, respectively.

In the pagan community various forms of neo-paganism can be quite different, having very different origins and, despite the shared name, these representations can vary quite considerably. Some celebrate in a manner as close as possible to how they believe ancient pagans observed the Summer Solstice, while others observe the holiday with rituals culled from numerous other unrelated sources, the Germanic culture being just one of those used. In neo-druidism, the term *Alban Hefin* is used for the Summer Solstice – a name invented by the late 18th-century Welsh Romantic author and prolific literary forger Iolo Morganwg.

Germanic neo-pagans call their Summer Solstice festival *Litha*, which is part of the reconstructed Germanic calendar and takes its name from Bede's *De temporum ratione* that provides Anglo-Saxon names for the months roughly corresponding to June and July as *sē ǣrra līþa* and *sē æfterra līþa* (the 'early Litha month' and the 'later Litha month') with an intercalary month of *līþa* appearing after *sē æfterra līþa* on leap years. In modern times, *Litha* is celebrated by neo-pagans who emphasize what they believe to be the reconstruction of Anglo-Saxon paganism's Wheel of the Year.

Midsummer's Eve, Swedish *Midsommarafton* and *Midsommar*, Finnish *Juhannus*, Danish *Sankt Hans Aften*, Norwegian

Sankhansaften, are holidays celebrating the longest day of the year in the Northern Hemisphere, the Summer Solstice (June 21st). Midsummer's Eve is observed in several countries and is a national holiday in Sweden and Finland. In Sweden the holiday is officially observed on a Friday between June 19th and 25th, whereas in Finland it is officially celebrated on a Saturday between June 20th and 26th – though festivities begin the preceding Friday evening. During this time many Scandinavians travel to rural parts of the country. Midsummer Eve activities in Sweden include gathering around a flower-festooned maypole (*majstång*) to sing and dance, an ancient custom probably relating to earlier fertility rites. Before the holiday Scandinavians thoroughly clean their houses and decorate them with flowers and other greenery. In Denmark holiday traditions include singing *Vi elsker vort land* ('We Love Our Land') and building a bonfire where a symbolic straw witch is sacrificed in remembrance of church-sanctioned witch burnings in the 16th and 17th centuries. Traditional foods, such as pickled herring, smoked fish, new potatoes, and strawberries, are served, along with beer and schnapps.

These celebrations predate Christianity and are likely related to ancient folk customs and ceremonies performed to ensure a successful harvest on land and sea. The holiday was later rededicated to honour Saint John the Baptist and although the meaning of the holiday has changed, a large number of pagan customs still persist, such as the bonfires, which originally were believed to ward off evil spirits, and the focus on Nature, which harkens back to when plants and water were thought to have magical healing powers on Midsummer Eve. [*Britannica*] Midsummer was considered to be a time of magic, and anything to do with Nature was thought to have that special power; gathering flowers to weave into wreaths and crowns was a way to harness Nature's magic to ensure good health throughout the year.

At the time of writing, we in the UK hadn't been permitted to spend a night away from home so last year's celebration of the Summer Solstice was restricted to a simple domestic affair: no watching the dawn come up behind a Stonehenge menhir for us. Instead we watched the rather lascivious *A Midsummer Night's Dream* from the BBC's Shakespeare Collection with Helen Mirren as Titania and Peter McEnery as Oberon, to get a taste of how Shakespeare and his early audiences greeted the height of summer in the late 16th-century.

The rites and habits associated with 'midsummer' clustered around a number of dates in Shakespeare's time; the Solstice occurred on a day between the 20th and 22nd June, but 'Midsummer Day' was fixed in the calendar as 24th (also known as St John's Day). Midsummer was one of the most popular and keenly-observed festivals throughout the early modern period. Rural communities marked it with Morris dancing, processions, late-night drinking, the blessing of crops and the ritual banishment of devils and other unwelcome sprites – precisely the sort of pagan-originating, Catholic-saint-encompassing mishmash that Protestant reformers despised.

Flinty-eyed provincial Puritans were particularly irritated by the giddiness of Midsummer Day because it had been barely more than a month since everyone had got up to the same sort of thing on May Day, the ancient celebration of spring that overlapped in many respects with the conventions of Midsummer. In Shakespeare's play, 'Maying' rituals seem to be on his mind despite the title: planning his elopement with Hermia, Lysander instructs her to meet him in the woods beyond Athens where he did 'meet thee once with Helena / To do observance to a morn of May'. Later in the play, when Theseus and his train discover the dishevelled lovers asleep in the forest, he concludes that 'they rose up early to observe / The rite of May'. [Shakespeare's Globe]

Perhaps it should also be mentioned that *Beltaine* is referred to in some of the earliest Irish/Celtic literature and is associated with important events in Irish mythology. Also known as *Cétshamhain* ('first of summer'), it marked the beginning of summer and was when cattle were driven out to the summer pastures.

Theseus is putting it decorously, but the 'rites of May' known to Shakespeare from his rural upbringing could take a turn for the raunchy. In *The Anatomy of Abuses* (1583), his assault on all sources of fun in late Elizabethan England, the religious reformer Philip Stubbes alerted his readers to the lewd goings-on in the country's summertime forests:

> *[On] May[day], Whitsunday or other time, all the young men and maids, old men and wives, run gadding over night to the woods, groves, hills, and mountains, where they spend all night in pleasant pastimes [...] And no marvel, for there is a great lord present amongst them, as superintendent over their pastimes and sports, namely Satan, Prince of Hell.*

That's not to say their passing wasn't marked. The pamphleteer Humphrey King, in a poem published early in the seventeenth century, honoured the 'May-Game Lords and Summer Queens' and 'milk-maids dancing o'er the greens' who ran afoul of local disapproval:

> *But I wonder now and then,*
> *To see the wise and learned men,*
> *With countenance grim, and many a frown,*
> *Cr[y], 'Masters, pluck the May-pole down!'*
> *To hear this news, the milk-maid cries;*
> *To see the sight the ploughman dies.*

Shakespeare evidently thought it important to bring rural culture onto the metropolitan stage, as we've seen from *The Merry Wives of Windsor* and *A Midsummer Night's Dream* at the start of his career to *The Winter's Tale* at the end, he found ways to weave country habits – Maying, Morris dancing, and midsummer madness – into plays written for urban spectators increasingly distant from the pre-Reformation ways of earlier generations. Stubbes regarded late-night summer partying as a time of dangerous sexual excess, when the usually strict rules of propriety and chastity were relaxed. Don't underestimate Stubbes's outrage in the phrase 'pleasant pastimes', which would have conjured up in Puritan minds a vision of devilish erotic adventurism. And if his warning of *al fresco* debauchery was a little over-heated, it was based on real behaviour. On holiday nights in May and June, men and women took advantage of mild temperatures and the privacy afforded by a shady grove to spend time together with a freedom that would have been impossible in day-to-day life. Like cultures the world over, pre-modern English people understood the significance of set times in the year when disorderly conduct was permitted – even encouraged – as long as the festive cycle concluded with a return to strait-laced 'normality'. [Shakespeare's Globe]

But, by the time Shakespeare wrote *A Midsummer Night's Dream*, May Day and Midsummer rituals were rare in large towns, they were gradually being abandoned in the countryside. Opposition from the church, and from bourgeois society concerned with respectability, put paid to the license of Midsummer. Shakespeare's neighbours in London were probably more likely to have watched a version of the rites of May in the theatre than to have participated themselves.

So ... the Summer Solstice, otherwise known as Midsummer, marks both the longest day and the shortest night of the year in the Northern Hemisphere, and is technically the official start of summer. According to the CultureTrip, it's also one of Europe's most celebrated and spiritual evenings, which has long been associated with both Christian as well as a more ancient pagan rituals. It's not just Europe that revels in longer days, however, so I've also featured many global locations in this line-up of the top Summer Solstice traditions.

Starting in Europe, Sweden is surely the unrivalled champion of midsummer celebrations. Their *'Midsommarstång'* festivities, marked by decadent indulgence and rooted in paganism, are some of the most important in this Scandinavian country's calendar, and which unite Swedes of all ages. Traditional foods such as pickled herring, salmon, and potatoes are enjoyed by flower-wreath-wearing revelers, and maypole and folk dances – such as the *Små grodorna* – take center stage. It's even said that if unmarried girls place seven flowers under their pillow on midsummer, they'll dream of their future husband.

Many customs also include burning a witch figure on top of the fire, usually made from straw and cloth, as it is believed that witches convene on solstice night. According to Danish folklore, this meeting occurs on Bloksbjerg, the Brocken mountain, and the burning 'sends the witch away'.

Is it unfair to lump Norway, Finland and Iceland under one entry? Probably. However, these three Nordic countries do share some remarkable similarities when it comes to celebrating the Summer Solstice. In Norway, enormous barrel bonfires are popular, and Finland (whose *'juhannus'* midsummer festivities were formerly based on the god Ukko before being John the Baptist-ized) similarly let loose to celebrate several extra hours of light by also crafting huge bonfires. Iceland, on the other hand, celebrates their twenty-one hours of daylight by throwing a huge three-day 'Secret Solstice Midnight Sun Music Festival'.

As we've seen, it's not surprising that the country in which Shakespeare's *A Midsummer Night's Dream* is based has some pretty typical Summer Solstice celebrations, especially given the UK's pagan past. Festivities in pre-Christian times focused on fairies, unicorns and other suitably mystical creatures, until Christianity duly stamped these traditions out! Nowadays, certain areas are reviving these processions and plays, while bonfires are still typical in Cornwall and Ireland. Naturally,

Stonehenge sees many druids and pagans coming to witness the perfectly aligned sunrise, too.

Latvia takes a leaf (no pun intended) out of Sweden's flower-wreath-wearing book at midsummer, also favoring the use of these now festival-friendly pieces of *floral* headwear for women and leafier versions for men. Known as Jāṇi (after John the Baptist), this special annual event is typically accompanied by plenty of parties, cheese, and beer, as well as some possibly ill-advised leaping over bonfires that are kept burning all night long. Traditional folk songs and cars decorated with branches sometimes make an appearance, too. People in Estonia and Latvia believe that the fire scares away mischievous harvest-ruining spirits, so the bigger the fire the further away the spirits keep (so the better the harvest will be). Estonians believe that *not* lighting a fire invites fire into the home, causing devastation. [CultureTrip]

In a similar vein, Jumping over the bonfire is a popular tradition in places such as Croatia, Lithuania, Latvia, Estonia, Russia and Spain. Bulgaria has its own version with their Enyovden celebration (taking place on 24th June), which they believe marks the start of winter. Participants join a fire ritual involving dancing on smouldering embers, called *Nestinarstvo*.

Bonfires and firework displays are popular in Spain when it comes to celebrating midsummer, and special beacons are ritualistically lit throughout the Pyrenees, in Spain, Andorra and France. Midsummer in that region is tied to feelings of belonging, and also marks a transition into adulthood for many adolescents. However, Spain in particular seems to celebrate more of a mish-mash between Christian culture and pagan ritual. The midsummer Festival of St. Joan festivities, particularly in Barcelona, Menorca, and other Catalan-speaking regions, prove especially popular. Celebrated on June 23rd and 24th each year, Sant Joan is a special date in the Catalan calendar which marks the Summer Solstice and the birth-date of Saint John the Baptist in the Christian faith. Crowds gather with anticipation for the colorful firework displays which light up the city the night before the *Dia de Sant Joan* when families gather for a slice of the special cake known as *coca de Sant Joan*.

Just as communities in the Pyrenees celebrate midsummer by lighting beacons, Austria comes together to light hundreds of mountain fires to mark this magical time. Stemming from a medieval tradition, it's thought that these fires were ways to worship the earth. Nowadays, revelers can make use of cable car systems to get a bird's eye view of the tradition, which is particularly popular in the Wilder Kaiser region of Tyrol, or simply head to Lake Achensee for a Summer Solstice cruise.

The USA is vast, and there are many different summer solstice celebrations which take place there on an annual basis. However, some of the most well-known include Times Square's day-long yoga event which sees hundreds of yoga fiends join together to practice the activity throughout the day. Alternatively, head to the zany Santa Barbara Summer Solstice parade which has a different theme year on year, or celebrate like a Swede in Battery Park, NYC instead.

Midsummer celebrations in Russia and Ukraine are remarkably similar to, and share many likenesses with, other European festivities, particularly the Latvian penchant for jumping over burning bonfires, although they also embrace skinny dipping. Other water-based activities common over the Summer Solstice include floating flower garlands in water and making predictions based on their movements. Known as Kupala Night or Ivan's Day in Russia and Ukraine, it has roots in pagan fertility festivals, but a name inspired by the Russian name for John the Baptist.

The bonfire is a recurring feature in almost all cultural celebrations. The central belief is that the fire deters evil spirits who roam freely as the sun turns south although most of the customs seem to be fairly recent innovations. In northern Europe, huge fires are lit on St. John's Eve, around which people dance and the custom goes right back to the 12th century. According to popular belief, it frightens off the evil spirits that cause illness and harm livestock, and averts storms. In some areas straw dolls are thrown into the fire, the practice known as *Hanslverbrennen*. And certain regions still uphold the custom of the *Johanniskrone*, a woven wreath or crown of twigs and leaves decorated with flowers and ribbons. In earlier times, the wreath was hung up on the village green and danced around every night until the greenery died.

The greater the difference between the fruitfulness of summer and the harshness of winter, the greater tends to be the significance of the Summer Solstice for the populations of the various countries. As a result, these northern Europe midsummer festivals are often the second most important celebration after Christmas. Even in southern Europe the longest day of the year is a cause for festivities: in Spain fires are lit along the beaches.

Collecting summer flowers and herbs on the Solstice evening, especially those believed to have potent medicinal properties, such as St John's Wort, are common activities. These bunches are hung in doorways or left in water overnight, to wash with the following morning. In many places, it is believed that anyone seeing the Solstice sunrise will be healthy throughout the year. Due to the belief that medical and magical herbs have more potency before dawn, witches go to gather herbs by sunrise to cure and make charms.

Because this is an important day in the Coven calendar it is vital to synchronize our working to the precise moment in order to periodically re-energise the 'group's solar mind'. And for this we chose to celebrate Mid-Summer and the Summer Solstice as one in accordance with the Old Ways. Since this marks the half-way stage of the agrarian year, the goddess-power will now slowly begin to wane and god-power gradually be on the increase until he fully comes into his own at the Autumnal Equinox.

The actual date and time of the Summer Solstice will vary slightly each year (for astronomical reasons) but this information can be checked well in advance on the internet. And since it is Mid-Summer, the rite should be held outside with the participants barefoot, since the Earth has natural electromagnetic waves, and when we stand barefoot on the ground an energy exchange also occurs to help with the re-energising of Coven members individually.

In *Wort-lore: The Craft of Witches*, I revealed that the names of plants used in witchcraft and spell-casting often had their own particular brand of magical 'short-hand', many being the old rural names by which they were known in different parts of the country. For example, this traditional rhyme has obviously been adapted at some stage from Shakespeare's *Macbeth*:

Round about the cauldron go
In! The herbs of magic throw,
Elfwort, trefoil, goat's leaf, bour,
In the cauldron the magic four.
Goatweed, basil, graveyard dust
Thrice about it go we must.
Elf-leaf, dilly, Juno's tears,
Witchbane, bat's wings, dead men's bells
Together bind this magic spell.
Thrice about the cauldron run,
Charm the spell and it be done.

It isn't difficult to see how mysterious and exotic these ingredients sound until it is shown that they are merely the old country names for plants used in spell-casting. For example, 'elfwort' is elecampane, a member of the sunflower family and its use goes back to ancient Greece; 'goat's leaf' is honeysuckle and 'bour' a 14th century name for elder flowers. 'Goatweed' refers to St John's wort and 'graveyard dust' to valerian. 'Elf-leaf' refers to either rosemary or lavender, and 'dilly' is the herb dill; 'Juno's tears' is vervain; 'witchbane' is rowan, 'bat's wings' is holly and 'dead men's bells' is foxglove.

To use these flowers for a protective pouch it is necessary to make a fresh one every year as part of the Mid-Summer Rite and burn the old one in the sacred (hearth) fire. All the ingredients for the new one must be harvested and dried at the time of the full moon around Midsummer's Eve. Once all the ingredients are assembled, circle your cauldron chanting: *'Round about the cauldron go ...'*

Contemporary celebrants develop their own rituals based around this fire festival, simply because most of the traditional ways of celebrating the Mid-Summer Festival have been abandoned and lost. *Sumer Is Icumen In* is a way of helping to restore an ancient way of observing one of the most important feasts of the Elder Faith by stripping away all the Christian contaminants and re-introducing some good, old-fashioned pagan revels!

Summer has come in
Sing loudly, cuckoo!
Seed grows and meadows bloom
And the wood springs forth anew.
Sing, cuccu!

The ewe bleats after the lamb
The cow lows after the calf
The bull leaps, the buck farts.
Murie sing, cuccu!
Cuccu, cuccu,

You sing well, cuccu.
Never be quiet now, ever!
Sing cuccu nu, sing cuccu!
Sing cuccu, sing cuccu nu!

16

Chapter Two

A Monumental Undertaking

In today's pagan litany, the many and varied folklore and customs are a tedious blend of simple peasant traditions that do nothing to reflect the deeply spiritual aspects that the Summer Solstice had for our Ancestors. If we turn to the mighty monuments of the past that were aligned with the rising or setting sun of the Mid-Summer Festival, we find ourselves observing with pride those gigantic earth-works and menhirs constructed under the guidance of a highly sophisticated astronomer-priesthood of the Neolithic Age. *This*, then is our pagan heritage and it's been going strong long before *our* high days and holy days were assimilated into the Church calendar.

For many people, the Summer Solstice is simply the first day of summer and the longest day of the year, meaning that it has more daylight hours than any other day. In the northern hemisphere, the Summer Solstice falls between June 20th and 22nd (In the southern hemisphere, it's in December.) But for some ancient civilizations, the Summer Solstice was a major yearly event – so much so that they built major constructions and monuments based on the sun's place in the sky on this particular day.

The word *solstice* comes from the Latin words *sol* (sun) and *stitium* (still or stopped). The Summer Solstice was such a big deal for people in ancient times because it marked the point of the year when the sun stopped moving northward in the sky and allowed them to start tracking its southward movement as summer turned to autumn. From a practical standpoint, the Summer Solstice meant that it was time to determine when to plant and harvest various crops, and the ancient architects who designed these incredible structures knew exactly what they were doing.

Let's start with the one everyone knows: Stonehenge located on Salisbury Plain in England and built in several stages. The first monument on the site was an early henge monument, built about 5,000 years ago but the stone circle most people think of when they think of Stonehenge was erected in the late Neolithic period, around 2500 BC, near some early Bronze Age burial mounds. Despite studying the site for hundreds of years, experts still aren't sure who, exactly, built Stonehenge – or why.

The main axis of the stones is aligned upon the solstitial axis, according to English Heritage, who cares for more than 400 historic buildings, monuments, and sites in England. 'At midsummer, the sun rises over the horizon to the northeast, close to the Heel Stone,' the English Heritage website explains. 'At midwinter, the sun sets in the southwest, in the gap between the two tallest trilithons, one of which has now fallen.' This prehistoric monument has long been studied for its possible connections with ancient astronomy. The site is aligned in the direction of the sunrise of the Summer Solstice and the sunset of the Winter Solstice and archaeoastronomers have made a range of further claims about the site's connection to astronomy, its meaning, and its use.

Stonehenge has an opening in the henge earthwork facing northeast, and suggestions that particular significance was placed by its builders on the solstice and equinox points have followed. For example, the Summer Solstice sun rose close to the Heel Stone, and the sun's first rays shone into the centre of the monument between the horseshoe arrangement. While it is possible that such an alignment could be coincidental, this astronomical orientation had been acknowledged since William Stukeley first identified its axis along the midsummer sunrise in 1720, noticing that the Heel Stone was not precisely aligned on the sunrise. The drifting of the position of the sunrise due to the change in the obliquity of the ecliptic since the monument's erection does not account for this imprecision. Recently, evidence has been found for a no longer extant neighbour to the Heel Stone. The second stone may have instead been one side of a 'solar corridor' used to frame the sunrise.

Although Stonehenge has become an increasingly popular destination during the Summer Solstice, with 20,000 people visiting in 2005, scholars have developed growing evidence that indicates prehistoric people visited the site only during the Winter Solstice. The only megalithic monuments in the 'Celtic' Isles to contain a clear, compelling solar alignment are Newgrange (Ireland) and Maeshowe (Orkney) which both famously face the Winter Solstice sunrise. The most recent evidence supporting the theory of winter visits includes bones and teeth from pigs which were slaughtered at nearby Durrington Walls, their age at death indicating that they were slaughtered either in December or January every year. Mike Parker Pearson of the University of Sheffield has said: 'We have no evidence that anyone was in the landscape in summer'.

Similarly, in Ireland and Britain, the Summer Solstice – also known as Midsummer – traditionally falls on June 21st each year and why do Irish people go to the Hill of Tara to celebrate it? In ancient pagan times in Ireland, the Summer Solstice symbolised that the power of the sun was at its highest and was believed to be a sacred time; held sacred by people from the Neolithic era the Hill of Tara was believed by worshippers to be a 'homeplace' of the gods and an entrance to the world of eternal joy. Every year on June 21st hundreds of people flock to the Hill in County Meath to mark the day and watch the sunrise.

Many towns and cities have traditional 'Midsummer Carnivals' with fairs, concerts and fireworks either on or at the weekend nearest to the Solstice. Midsummer bonfires have also been a tradition in Ireland for hundreds of years. In rural spots particularly to Ireland's northwest, the bonfires are lit on hilltops; a tradition that harks back to pagan times and is now associated with St. John's Night.

A few miles away, Newgrange is best known for the illumination of its passage and chamber by the *Winter Solstice* sun. Above the entrance to the passage of the mound there is an opening called a roof-box and on mornings around the Winter Solstice a beam of light penetrates the roof-box and travels up the 19-metre passage and into the inner chamber. As the sun rises higher, the beam widens so that the whole chamber is dramatically illuminated as golden fingers of sunlight creep slowly through the opening; the rays pouring into the inner chamber, illuminating it completely for a few magical moments.

The Carrowkeel cairns are in the Bricklieve Mountains in County Sligo. Cairn G also has a roof-box above the entrance, similar to Newgrange. The sun enters the chamber at sunset on the days around the Summer Solstice, illuminating the back of the chamber. Carrowkeel Cairn G is estimated to be 700 years older than Newgrange; it is smaller and less sophisticated, the passage being only two meters long compared with nineteen metres at Newgrange. The Summer Solstice was seen as a time to banish evil spirits, through the light of the sun and the ancient people of Ireland would use this time to pray for a good harvest, as it was halfway through the growing season. The Solstice was also seen as a time of change, nature, and new beginnings. It was also associated with fertility.

Bryn Celli Ddu is a prehistoric site on the island of Anglesey located near Llanddaniel Fab. Its name means 'the mound in the dark grove'. It was archaeologically excavated between 1928 and 1929. Visitors can get inside the mound through a stone passage to the burial chamber, and it is the centre-piece of a major Neolithic Scheduled Monument in the care of Cadw. The presence of a mysterious pillar within the burial chamber, the reproduction of the 'Pattern Stone', carved with sinuous serpentine designs, and the fact that the site was once a henge with a stone circle – and may have been used to plot the date of the Summer Solstice – have all attracted academic interest.

An excavation continues on the site of a suspected 4,500-year-old burial cairn that lies next to one of Wales' most important prehistoric monuments. Experts are hoping to learn more about it and its relationship to the Bryn Celli Ddu burial chamber – a 5,000-year-old 'passage tomb' aligned to coincide with the rising sun on the Summer Solstice.

Dr Ffion Reynolds said the cairn showed the site remained a 'special location' centuries after the chamber was built, since more recent excavations have shown human activity around the site throughout history, suggesting that Bronze Age people were coming back to the same location as their Neolithic ancestors and adding their own mark to the landscape. Excavations have shown the burial chamber was built as a henge – a ritual enclosure like Stonehenge – consisting of a bank around an inner ditch, enclosed in a circle of upright stones. The passage tomb was added later. One of the most striking discoveries was the giant decorated pattern stone found near a ceremonial pit at the rear of the chamber. The site as a whole appeared to be 'dedicated to the ancestors', according to Dr Reynolds from Cadw, the Welsh Government's historic environment service.

If we travel further north, we discover the world explored by Pytheas the Greek of the 'islands of the Pretanni' with their spectacular monuments that suggests these northern islands had been, at one time, an important cultural and religious centre for many thousands of years prior to his arrival. He wrote an account of his journey – *On the Ocean* – which he published on his return to safety in 320BC – of the far limit of literate human experience in the northern world.

Around 3000BC, the local communities had developed a refined interest in astronomy, building circles of upstanding stones on Lewis and Orkney and spectacular chambered tombs such as Maeshowe on Orkney that were aligned with the setting sun on the midwinter solstice. People with these abilities, who had acquitted

through experiment and long observation an intimate knowledge
of celestial phenomena, were astronomers in their own right ...
anyone who has looked at the sophistication of Maeshowe and
considered the domineering belief that drove people to erect the
Stones of Stenness, or the circle and alignments of Callanish cannot
fail to wonder at the innovative power of the local elites at this time.
[Barry Cunliffe]

The surviving Stones of Stenness are sited on a promontory at the
south bank of the stream that joins the southern ends of the sea
Loch of Stenness and the freshwater Loch of Harray. The name,
which is pronounced *stane-is* in Orcadian dialect, comes from
Old Norse meaning *stone headland*. The stream is now bridged,
but at one time was crossed by a stepping stone causeway, and
the Ring of Brodgar lies about 0.75 mile away to the north-
west, across the stream and near the tip of the isthmus formed
between the two lochs. Maeshowe chambered cairn is about 0.75
mile to the east of the Standing Stones of Stenness and several
other Neolithic monuments also lie in the vicinity, suggesting
that this area had particular importance.

Thought to date from 2500 BC the stones of Ring of Brodgar,
also known as the Temple of the Sun, align with sunset and
sunrise on the solstices. In June, night is brief on Scotland's
Orkney Islands – the sun dips only barely below the horizon,
creating an overnight period of twilight known locally as 'simmer
dim'. So expect a very early wake-up call (or late night) if you want
to celebrate Summer Solstice.

Perhaps the best-known attribute of Maeshowe, however, is
its world-famous midwinter alignment. In the weeks leading up
to the Winter Solstice, the darkest time of the Orcadian year, the
last rays of the setting sun shine through Maeshowe's entrance
passage to pierce the darkness of the chambered cairn. Theories
abound as to the significance of this phenomenon, explains
orkneyjar.com:

- Just as the death of the midwinter sun marked the return of life, did its entry into the tomb symbolise the continuance of the 'life' of those who had died and had been placed within?
- Did the entry of the sun represent rebirth, or a fertility rite of some sort?
- Was the shaft of sunlight thought to carry away the souls of the dead? Or perhaps return them?
- Or was it simply a calendar to remind the ancient Orcadians that the darkest time of the year had passed and that the light was once again returning?

In truth, we will never fully know the answer, although we can be fairly certain that it marked the passing of time – the death of the old year and the birth of the new one – and was an indicator that the days were lengthening again. To the users of Maeshowe, just as it still does today, the return of the sun heralded a resurgence of light and the return of life to the land. Although in Orkney the worst of winter often follows the Winter Solstice, to this day it remains a comforting thought to know the days are lengthening again.

But although we can only speculate as to the purpose of the alignment, what is clear is the skill of the Neolithic architects and builders who designed and built Maeshowe. Not only did they raise the remarkable structure, but it was built precisely to allow the light at the darkest point of the year to illuminate their house of the dead. Although the common conception is that Maeshowe's alignment is connected specifically to the day of the Winter Solstice, the truth is that the cairn is illuminated for a number of weeks on either side of the shortest day.

Key to this event is a connection between the howe and the nearby solitary monolith, known as the Barnhouse Stone. Around the Winter Solstice, the sun sets over the top of the Stone, its last rays going on to illuminate the darkness of Maeshowe's inner chamber. At first this alignment was thought to be purely coincidental but later excavations around Maeshowe uncovered a socket at the tomb's entrance that appears to have at one time housed a standing stone, similar to the one at Barnhouse. It has now been shown that the centre axis of the inner entrance passage is directly aligned with the centre of the Barnhouse Stone. From here, the line travels out to strike Hoy's Ward Hill, at a place where the sun sets 22 days before, and after, the midwinter solstice.

Recent research at Maeshowe revealed another interesting solar phenomenon – a period when the setting sun briefly reappears from the side of Hoy's Ward Hill before disappearing beneath the horizon. This phenomenon has been called 'flashing', from the flashes of light apparent seen within the cairn. The phenomenon of the midwinter solstice and its relevance to Orkney's most famous chambered cairn has captured the imagination of Orcadians from time immemorial. The late George Mackay Brown penned what is perhaps the most poignant account of the event:

The most exciting thing in Orkney, perhaps in Scotland, is going to happen this afternoon at sunset, in few other places even in Orkney can you see the wide hemisphere of sky in all its plenitude. The winter sun just hangs over the ridge of the Coolags. Its setting will seal the shortest day of the year, the winter solstice. At this season the sun is a pale wick between two gulfs of darkness. Surely there could be no darker place in the be-wintered world than the interior of Maeshowe. One of the light rays is caught in this stone web of death. Through the long corridor it has found its way; it splashes the far wall of the chamber. The illumination lasts a few minutes, then is quenched. Winter after winter I never cease to wonder at the way primitive man arranged, in hewn stone, such powerful symbolism. [Orkneyjar.com]

The Callanish Stones are situated on a low ridge above the waters of Loch Roag with the hills of Great Bernera as a backdrop on the Isle of Lewis. Numerous other ritual sites lie within a few kilometres. These include at least three other circles, several arcs, alignments and single stones; many visible from the main site. The most impressive – Callanish II and Callanish III – lie just over a kilometre southeast of the main Callanish Stones, and originally consisted of circles of stones at least eight in number. The existence of other monuments in the area implies that Callanish was an active focus for prehistoric religious activity for at least 1500 years and Historic Environment Scotland states that the stones were erected roughly 5,000 years ago, pre-dating Stonehenge by at least 2,000 years.

According to one tradition, the Callanish Stones were petrified giants who would not convert to Christianity. In the 17th century the people of Lewis were calling the stones *fir bhrèige* ('false men'), while another legend is that early on midsummer morning an entity known as the 'Shining One' walks the length of the avenue, his coming heralded by the call of the cuckoo.

Recently, researchers have found statistical proof that the earliest standing stone monuments in Britain, called the great circles, were specifically constructed 5,000 years ago to line up with the movements of the sun and the moon. These strange structures, erected in two locations in Scotland, pre-date Stonehenge by some 500 years, and initiated a 2,000-year-long practice of building astronomical monuments in the region.

Nobody before this has ever statistically determined that a single stone circle was constructed with astronomical phenomena in mind – "it was all supposition," says project leader Gail Higginbottom from the University of Adelaide. "This research is finally proof that the ancient Britons connected Earth to the sky with their earliest standing stones, and that this practice continued in the same way for 2000 years."

Higginbottom and her team examined the oldest great stone circles built in Britain – one in the village of Callanish, on the Isle of Lewis, and one in the village of Stenness, on the Isle of Orkney. These great circles were likely constructed around 3000 to 2900 BC, using tall, thin slabs of stone. To get a better idea of what they would have originally looked like, the team created 3D landscape models of the circles, plus the surrounding landscape and the astronomical phenomena that would have been circling above. Using these, they discovered that the sites share a combination of astronomical and landscape cues that were also found at smaller Bronze Age sites built more than 1,500 years later, on the nearby Scottish islands of Coll, Tiree, and Mull.

So the evidence suggests that 5,000 years ago, the ancient people of Scotland had managed to weave the sky and the land together in their stone circles to reflect the complex movements of the lunar and solar cycles at different stages, and this practice was continued for at least another two millennia elsewhere in the country.

"These people chose to erect these great stones very precisely within the landscape and in relation to the astronomy they knew. They invested a tremendous amount of effort and work to do so," says Higginbottom. "It tells us about their strong connection with their environment, and how important it must have been to them, for their culture and for their culture's survival." [Journal of Archaeological Science]

Needless to say, there are many other monuments in the ancient world that are celestially aligned and although the Pyramids get all the press, there's another incredible architectural wonder in Egypt built around the light of the Summer Solstice. The Temple of Karnak in Luxor is the modern-day name for the ancient site of the Temple of Amun in what was formerly known as

Thebes. Ancient Egyptians believed that Thebes was the first city founded on the primordial mound that rose from the waters when the world was created. The Temple of Karnak was built on the site where the mound was thought to have been located, and it served as both a center of worship and an observatory. Dedicated to Amun, the god of sun and air, the temple was designed so that the inner sanctum – as well as its western gate – was perfectly aligned with sunset at the Summer Solstice, as priests interpreted this beam of light as the will of the god and his wishes for humanity.

Though most people may associate pyramids with Egypt, there are some spectacular structures in Mexico as well. One example of that is the Pyramid of Chichen Itza, which is about a two-and-a-half-hour drive from Cancún. Chichen Itza was the ancient capital of the Yucatán Maya, and as a result, it is home to an array of impressive structures, including its pyramid. Built between 800 and 900 CE, the Pyramid was designed to be aligned with the Summer Solstice. Over the course of five hours on the longest day of the year, a combination of light and shadows creates seven triangles on the side of the staircase. And for 45 minutes, it appears as though a serpent is crawling down the side of the temple. The pyramid is dedicated to Kukulcan (or Quetzalcoatl), the feathered serpent god, and according to legend, it was designed so that it appears as though the serpent visits the monument during the Summer and Winter Solstices.

In addition to the Pueblo-built sandstone buildings of Chaco Canyon, the state is also home to the Aztec Ruins National Monument, located in the town of Aztec. Ancestral Pueblo people had a strong relationship with the cosmos, and they built the back (north) wall of the monument so that it is perfectly aligned with the rising and setting sun as it touches the horizon during both the Summer and Winter Solstices. Despite its name, the Aztec Ruins National Monument was not built by the Aztec people (that was just an incorrect guess from early settlers) but instead by the ancestral Puebloans, taking around 200 years to build the structures, which date from around the 12th century.

The ancient city of Machu Picchu is the most-visited tourist attraction in Peru and located in this Incan city is the Temple of the Sun, one of the site's most sacred temples. One of the temple's windows, shaped like a trapezoid, was positioned along the curve of the wall of the solar observatory to capture sunlight during the solstice in June (which in Peru happens to be the Winter Solstice). In addition, there are two windows in the section of the temple used for sacrifices that align with both the Summer and Winter solstices. The Incas worshipped and believed themselves descendants of the sun and so, in the semi-circular Temple of the Sun, they built a window so that on the Winter Solstice the sun would shine through it and light a specific spot carved on a sacred rock. A similar window is found in the Temple of the Sun in Cuzco, the ruins of which form the foundation of the Santo Domingo Church, a colonial structure that, though built by the Spanish, incorporates Inca stonework.

Nearer to home and located on the island of Malta, the Mnajdra Temple was built 5,500 years ago to align with both the Summer and Winter Solstices. Technically, there are three temple units in Mnajdra, set around a curved forecourt, placed next to one another to form a semicircle. The first temple is the oldest, and it is in the shape of a simple trefoil and made out of stone. One of the stones has what some think looks like a calendar on it, though there is no hard evidence that it is. The second temple was built next and is thought to have been an observatory. In this building, the sun enters the structure directly through the doorway and lights up a spot at the back center of the temple. Malta is also home to two temples that are among the oldest buildings in the world.

Perhaps one of the most magnificent alignments, however, is that of the Pantheon in Rome – the best-preserved architectural monument of the Imperial period and built to honour all the gods. Originally built by Agrippa around 27BC under Augustus's rule, it was destroyed by fire under Domitian, then rebuilt and finally completed in its present form during Hadrian's reign, in c.AD128. There is a great deal of uncertainty about the original Agrippan design; excavations, however, have suggested that this building was already circular (although probably open to the sky) and orientated in the same direction, in order to capture the longest day of the year and the exact moment when the sun perfectly aligns with the oculus at the Summer Solstice, sending a beam inside and illuminating the space.

Most of Rome's ancient religious buildings were designed with dark or dimly lit internal spaces, so entering the Pantheon with the light streaming in from above, the view skyward from below would have been a magical moment. On this date, the sun is directly over the Tropic of Cancer so it is the one day of the year when the sun shines down through the oculus and hits the floor not exactly directly down onto the centre but in front of the entrance – and where the Emperor would have made his grand entrance!

These architectural wonders make a timeless statement about how important the Summer Solstice was to the people of the Ancient World and no matter how many attempts were made to destroy them, they have withstood the ravages of time and desecration. We therefore owe it to our Ancestors to observe the Summer Solstice and make it holy.

Chapter Three

The Celebration

So ... since prehistory, the Summer Solstice has been seen as a significant time of year in many cultures, and has been marked by diverse festivals and rituals. According to the astronomical definition of the seasons, the summer solstice also marks the beginning of summer, which lasts until the Autumnal Equinox (22nd or 23rd September). Traditionally, the Summer Solstice is seen as the *middle* of summer, hence being referred to as 'the Midsummer festival'.

It is also one of the important fire festivals in the pagan calendar and we may have to re-think how we are going to re-introduce this observance into our celebrations. In view of the social changes wreaked by the Covid pandemic, we may also have to change the way we celebrate in the future *per se* ... so, not a bad time to re-organise our approach to this ancient festival. Like a lot of pagan festivals, this is a 'moveable feast' in that it rarely falls on the same day in consecutive years and could (if necessary) be arranged for a day at the nearest weekend.

The Cross Quarter Days or Fire Festivals of *Imbolc, Lammas, Samhain* and *Beltaine* were probably aligned with the solstices and equinoxes before precession and the various calendar changes moved things around. The term 'quarter days' is derived from a system in the British Isles in which certain days, falling four times a year, and probably near the solstice and equinox dates, were marked as a time to collect rents, hire new servants, and resolve legal matters. In England and Wales, the original quarter days were Lady Day, Midsummer, Michaelmas, and Christmas going back to the Middle Ages and which often remain a focal point in traditional British Old Craft calendar.

Some Wiccan traditions call the festival *Litha*, a name

occurring in Bede's *The Reckoning of Time* (*De Temporum Ratione*, 8th century), which preserves a list of the (then-obsolete) Anglo-Saxon names for the twelve months. *Ærra Liða* (*first* or *preceding Liða*) roughly corresponds to June in the Gregorian calendar, and *Æfterra Liða* (*following Liða*) to July. Bede writes that 'Litha means *gentle* or *navigable*, because in both these months the calm breezes are gentle and they were wont to sail upon the smooth sea'. Modern Druids celebrate this festival as *Alban Hefin*. The sun in its greatest strength is greeted and celebrated on this holiday. While it is the time of greatest strength of the solar current, it also marks a turning point, for the sun also begins its time of decline as the wheel of the year turns. Arguably the most important festival of the Druid traditions, due to the great focus on the sun and its light as a symbol of divine inspiration.

Litha is a pagan holiday; one of their eight sabbats during the year (also known as Midsummer) occurring on the Summer Solstice, and celebrating the beginning of summer. The traditions of *Litha* appear to be borrowed from many cultures and American academic and Wiccan, Aidan Kelly, gave names to the summer solstice (*Litha*) and equinox holidays (*Ostara* and *Mabon*) of Wicca in 1974. These were subsequently popularized by Timothy Zell through his *Green Egg* magazine, although the assimilation of these names only happened gradually within the modern traditions and ignored completely by the older ones.

Traditionally, this is an outdoor event but as the British summer is said to consist of three fine days and a thunderstorm, we can't guarantee good weather for our garden party even in June! A wide range of inexpensive garden furniture can help to minimize the damage by providing a gazebo or mini-marquee for the day or night because it doesn't matter where in the world you are, you can bet that, as soon as you set a date for a garden party, the weather misbehaves. So, I'd always advise preparing ahead for rain *and* shine. Gazebos are great, parasols look pretty and are forever useful and sail-shades are a quick fix but do make sure there's enough shelter for all or your guests will be huddled into a small dry patch like wet hens.

And, in case it *doesn't* rain, it's always a good idea to create a shaded area at your garden party for people who don't like being in the sun for too long, or if your guests want a shaded spot to relax away from the main event. A parasol would do the job, but, increasingly, people are loving sail-shades; they are just so simple and stylish and add a bit of a beachy vibe to a garden. Except if you live in the Glen where 40mph winds are not unknown throughout the summer months.

And, as this is a fire festival, a 'bonfire' is a must in the form of a patio fire basket or *chiminea* – but not under cover! Stylish fire pits enhance outdoor living by adding cosiness and warmth to the garden and are perfect for extending alfresco get-togethers late into the night. It also means we can carry on entertaining in the garden right into autumn. Not only does a fire pit provide warmth once the day's sun has gone down, it can change the aesthetics of our home and give our garden a wonderful warm glow. The most under-used room in the house is often the garden, but when we have a fire pit, there's no excuse that it's too cold when we can sit next to those flames in the still of the night and celebrate *all* of the fire festivals.

Needless to say, this Summer Solstice post-pandemic event is more than likely going to be a small(ish) family (or open) affair so we don't need to worry about any overt pagan symbolism as it's just a 'summer solstice get-together' ... but we still need to add a little touch of ambience, which comes from a French word meaning 'surrounding', and refers to the mood or atmosphere of a certain environment from table settings and mood lighting to ways to keep warm/cool.

A Mid-summer party can be as lavish or modest as we choose it can also be a time to catch up with people we haven't seen for a long time. Renew old friendships and introduce some new ones as mingling the crowd ensures that incompatible people aren't stuck with each other for the whole evening. This is a time for sun and lightness and any entertainment or theme should reflect this sentiment. If the budget can run to it, an outdoor firework display can be just as pleasurable after dark at mid-summer as it is on a wet, fog-bound November evening.

The Midsummer Day Garden Party

A lemonade or Pimm's stand is a fantastic addition for hot summer parties spent outdoors. And if we set up a pretty stand with lots of colourful flowers, our guests will happily serve themselves. Nothing screams 'garden party' like a lemonade dispenser. Plus it adds such a homely rustic feel to a garden party. We can pick them up really cheaply on Amazon and make our own lemonade really easily using just lemons, sugar and water. To whip up another delectably, lightly-spiced of beverages – take a jug and fill it with ice, mix one-part Pimm's with three parts chilled lemonade, add some mint, cucumber, orange and strawberry and we're good to go!

Serve up platters of finger food and sliced fresh fruit so everyone can dive in easily. Don't fancy doing lots of cooking for your garden party? Especially if we'll be hosting it on a small patio or terrace, where big plates of food might not be practical. Instead, serve a chic cheese and charcuterie board that people can dip in and out of as they choose. Keep it simple.

And keep the prepared food in a cool place until it's ready to be served by using small plates that can be often be replenished. To ensure our food doesn't spoil, it should not be left at room temperature for longer than two hours. This will be less if serving it outdoors on a hot day. Insulated storage containers are a no-nonsense way to keep food cold while doubling as serving dishes.

If we don't need to, don't lay all the food out at once. Stagger servings and/or portions so food won't be left sitting out unnecessarily. Appetizers and snacks first such as finger foods or a charcuterie board, then salads and any main dishes, followed by desserts, especially summer desserts. If you have a crowd, try to only put out portions of things like creamy potato salads/coleslaw (if you really can't do without them) and replenish as needed. Nothing looks less appetizing than wilting lettuce and melting mayonnaise!

An easy way to up your garden party game and make it feel like a special occasion is to simply lay down some lovely old table linen. You want to blur the lines between indoors and outdoors and make the tables outside feel just as special as they would at an indoor party. Layer a few vintage table clothes on top of one another for a laid back, rustic feel and match your table decor to that country vibe with wooden chopping boards instead of paper plates.

Make sure all table accessories co-ordinate and go for bright summer colours with plates that are large enough to hold an ample selection of finger food without overloading and don't automatically buckle if holding more than two canapés and a devilled egg! Provide plenty of good quality matching napkins for sticky fingers, and don't forget the ubiquitous rubbish bin tarted up with some floral self-adhesive stickers.

If we're looking to decorate our garden party ideas on a budget, then how about this simple idea that's ideal for giving a lift to foldaway chairs and is oh-so-easy to recreate. All we need is a handful of brightly-coloured lengths of ribbon. They will look gorgeous as they flutter in the breeze and will add an instant summery feel to any space. Finish the look with tie-on cushions for an extra dose of vibrancy and to up the comfy factor.

Decorating our garden with balloons adds an instant celebratory touch whatever the occasion, especially if we choose clear ones that have been pre-filled with sparkly confetti for a stylish look. Sticking to one design or a single colour makes more of a statement and is a great way of dressing up an outdoor space.

Bunting strung up beneath trees or along fences also adds to the sense of occasion. Or add streamers of coloured *papel picado,* 'perforated paper', a decorative craft made by cutting elaborate designs into sheets of tissue paper and considered a Mexican folk art. With countless combinations of patterns and colors, there are many different types of *papel picados* used in Mexican celebrations. Specific patterns are believed to hold significant meaning and worldly influence with the design that is cut into a *papel picado* being determined by the particular event at which it is displayed. Search out papel picado online for suppliers.

Keep an eye on the time. Guests invited to a daytime event have a tendency to outstay their welcome unless we add a specific time. For example:

Celebrate the First Day of Summer
with Carol and John
on the afternoon of Sunday 20th June.

But stock up with plenty of pizza or lasagna in the freezer just in case they don't want to go home ...

A Midsummer Night Party

If, however, we do want to make sure our garden party continues seamlessly into the evening, we need to prepare with plenty of outdoor lighting. Mix and match different types, from tea lights to lanterns, for a really pretty, luminous effect. Choose a selection of ambient lighting to add that all-important glow at dusk – the evening garden needs lots of lights to get the right effect. For the best results add layers of lighting at different heights. Start with tea lights in glass jars and hurricane lights at table height, then add festoon lights looped through the branches of shrubs, around pergolas or trellis and along fences. These glass-blown outdoor lamps add a sophisticated touch to any outdoor space. Whether we choose to arrange them individually or grouped together they will add drama to the night time garden that's perfect for parties.

Play with the lighting. Up-lighting on trees, soft glows of candles, twinkling lights on table tops and hanging votives all create a magical atmosphere and can help to zone different areas if the garden is big enough. Wrap floral arrangements or ivy around candelabras and suspend lanterns from branches and wrap fairy lights around trees.

Midsummer is the perfect time for parties. Take inspiration from Shakespeare's tale of a *Midsummer Night's Dream* with an enchanted woodland where we can create a magical world for our guests to enjoy. The food for our party should be light, fresh and simple. Think snacks rather than an actual formal meal. We want to create the lazy and luxurious feel of reclining and savoring the night away. Nuts, apricots and blackberries, figs, purple grapes, honey and cheese are all mentioned in the play.

Our reclining area should be arranged around the fire pit or basket because our guests probably share our beliefs and this is often the type of occasion that lapses into spontaneous magical discussions. These are the times that years down the line someone will always say: *'Hey, do you remember that night ...'* This is when we let the magic of the Solstice weave its own spell because in all honesty, it needs no extra input from us.

For this night we pay homage to our Ancestors who kept the Elder Faith alive, and whose geometric and astronomical skills created those Summer Solstice 'temples' and identified many stone alignments indicating prominent features on the horizon that marked the sun at the solstices and equinoxes. These solstitial alignments can also be seen as displays of ancestral power.

When viewed from a ceremonial plaza on the Island of the Sun (the mythical origin place of the Sun) in Lake Titicaca, for example, the sun was seen to rise at the June solstice between two towers on a nearby ridge. The sacred part of the island was separated from the remainder by a stone wall and ethnographic records indicate that access to the sacred space was restricted to members of the Inca ruling elite. Ordinary pilgrims stood on a platform outside the ceremonial area to see the solstice Sun rise between the towers.

Similarly, the temple of Karnak shows an impressive axis of symmetry which can certainly be interpreted in a context where astronomy combines with religion, history, and landscape to produce one of the most sacred traditional spots on Earth. Luxor's ancient temple complex is illuminated within by the rays of the rising sun in an event that occurs twice each year, on the Summer and Winter Solstices at the site of the primordial Mound which rose from the waters of chaos at the beginning of the world. At that time, the creator-god Atum stood on the mound to begin the work of creation.

Although the oldest standing building remains are only from the 12th Dynasty, and most of the original temple compound now lies under the modern city of Luxor and therefore currently inaccessible by archaeologists, the earliest evidence so far dates as far back as 3,200 BC. Sir Norman Lockyer proposed a Midsummer sunset alignment of the Main Axis of the Great Temple of Amon-Re (*The Dawn of Astronomy*, 1894). The temple has been the subject of much study, and evaluation of the site, taking into account the change over time of the obliquity of the ecliptic show that the Great Temple was also aligned on the rising of the Midwinter Sun. The length of the corridor down which sunlight would travel would have limited illumination at other times of the year.

In a later period, the Serapeum in Alexandria was also said to have contained a solar alignment so that, on a specific sunrise, a shaft of light would pass across the lips of the statue of Serapis thus symbolising the Sun saluting the god. Writing in AD402, Rufinus says: 'On the day that an image of the sun was to be carried into the Serapeum, a small window allowed a ray of sunlight to fall on the lips of the statue in a kiss of renewal, the image itself suspended in the air, as if by magic, by hidden magnets.'

Another solar alignment where the sun illuminates the face of the statue of Ramses II in the Temple of Abu Simbel and which is considered a major event in Egyptian history – holds many secrets of the pharaohs. Twice a year, the sun illuminates the face of the Pharaoh, passing along a 197-feet passage until it reaches the Holy of Holies. The sun also passes over the statue for 20-25 minutes at dawn of Oct. 22nd, which coincides with the start of the flood and agricultural season in ancient Egypt. On Feb. 22nd, the sun announces the start of the harvest season.

These are all ancient symbols of the Old Ways that *are* carved in stone and have survived the desecration and destruction of the incoming monotheistic religions that were hell-bent on eradicating the powerful beliefs of the solar-cult. Our Mid-summer night party allows us to acknowledge the fact that so strong are these links to the past, they have endured through 2000-years of persecution with enough of the belief intact to instigate a powerful pagan revival that grows in strength with each passing year. *So mote it be!*

As our Summer Solstice devotions focus on the fire pit-basket we have to admit that we get more heat from it by enclosing the surrounding area. Rebecca Newsom, head of Greenpeace politics, says:

The ideal technology for keeping warm outdoors without heating the entire atmosphere is still a jumper. There are a few other options. You could put up a windbreak, awning or gazebo to try to limit wind chill. In terms of clothing, you could invest in a good base layer in merino, bamboo or recycled yarn, wear two pairs of socks and liners inside your gloves, and dress head to toe for the climate where you live. Invest in a recycled insulated camping blanket, or unzip a sleeping bag and use it as a comforter. Make up some flasks and wrap your hands around a hot mug. Layer up until you can barely move. Dig out your old hot-water bottle, or if you don't have one, treat yourself to a recyclable model.

Hot food is often more appropriate for a chilly summer evening and although not as ambrosial as our *Midsummer Night's Dream* pickies, this is where the old slow-cooker comes into its own for curries or a spag bol that needs to be kept on stand-by for an indefinite time. Served with crusty bread and a robust red wine, this is the perfect libation to offer for a Summer Solstice night.

Give it a try. And, have an assortment of wraps and throws available in case the evening gets chilly and your less well-prepared guests look as though they might be succumbing to hyperthermia. If the cold is really unbearable ... then it's time to move indoors!

A Quiet Five-Minutes

When our guests have gone, we should allow ourselves a quiet five-minutes to make our own *obsequences* to the Old Ones as befits the occasion. As we know, at one time the Mid-Summer festival coincided with the Summer Solstice but with the Church's mania for aligning saints with sinners (i.e. the church calendar with pagan festivals), Mid-Summer Day was 'adjusted' to fall on St John's Day ... and then the old Julian calendar was replaced by the Gregorian version.

The Summer Solstice marks the moment during the year when the path of the Sun in the sky is farthest north in the Northern Hemisphere (20th or 21st June) or farthest south in the Southern Hemisphere (21st or 22nd December). According to the astronomical definition of the seasons, the Summer Solstice also marks the beginning of summer, which lasts until the Autumnal Equinox (22nd or 23rd September in the Northern Hemisphere, or 20th or 21st March in the Southern). So, in Old Craft, St John the Baptist and his Christian cohorts get booted into touch!

Because this is an important day in the Coven calendar it is vital to synchronize our working to the precise moment in order to periodically re-energise the 'group's solar mind'. And for this we choose to celebrate Mid-Summer's Eve and the Summer Solstice as one in accordance with the Old Ways. Since this marks the half-way stage of the agrarian year, the goddess-power will now slowly begin to wane and god-power gradually be on the increase until he fully comes into his own at the Autumnal Equinox.

The actual date and time of the Summer Solstice will vary slightly each year (for astronomical reasons) but this information can be checked well in advance on the internet. And since it is Mid-Summer, the rite should be held outside with the participants barefoot, since the Earth has natural electromagnetic waves, and when we stand barefoot on the ground an energy exchange also occurs to help with the re-energising of the Coven members individually.

For anyone of pagan persuasion left at our party for the pouring of the libation, there should also be a small platter of bread and salt to be passed around. According to tradition, a large round loaf on a towel or linen napkin is offered with a salt shaker on top. The guests should carefully break off a piece of the bread, dip it in the salt, and eat – this signals that a friendship has been forged or re-affirmed between host and guest. Within our Coven practice it is included as part of every Sabbat ritual to re-affirm the bonds of loyalty within the group and is non-negotiable!

If we casually integrate our pagan customs within our entertainments for the benefit of family and friends, we are breathing new life into our beliefs and helping to spread them among a new generation of party-goers. Nothing needs to have an 'in-your-face' approach but there's always a certain degree of satisfaction in knowing our guests are often paying court to the Old Ways without intending to.

It's also a time, however, to reflect on Dr Jerry Killingsworth's observation that we have so many values in our 'cultural truths' that are leading us towards 'a machine-artificial pagan intelligence and away from our customary values in religion and philosophy, and especially away from the primal traditions and perspectives'. We are beginning to suffer from a metaphysical ailment and that is the realization that our lives – with all our having and knowing – seems fragmented, separated and meaningless in the real sense of 'being'. In *Spiritual Reality*, he explains that there is evidence that many of us still believe that 'having' can replace 'being'. That explanation can replace experience; techno-singularity can replace the seamless web of existence, and that religion and philosophy can replace the mythical, the spiritual and the reality of direct experience, based on a tribal-identity immersed in and close to Nature.

We can see that the trivialized approach to Summer Solstice celebrations has debased the ancestral/tribal identity of this time of year when mighty, megalithic monuments were raised to honour the glory of our ancient gods and our ancestors. In our quiet five-minutes, we may have to reconsider those *tribal* traditions and their respect for all of life and the reciprocal relationship they had with the natural world. And, the reality of wholeness and unity, as compared with our modern pace of life and self-centered focus on self-aggrandisement and gratification. Perhaps it *is* time to turn the clock back to a time in our transition before we lost the mythical way of being spiritual to the scientific method of knowing 'truth' in terms of instant, repetitive, on-line knowledge.

While this is, obviously, an unscholarly generalization, it will serve my purpose of claiming that our great gains in civilisation have been in our religion, philosophy and science – but that these gains have come at a price, and the gains are obvious and visible … In my view the gains have been in the physical, material, technical, organizational, and if I may repeat: these are founded on believing, thinking, knowing and having … but what we have lost is in the mystical, holistic, experimental, spiritual, reality and living close to our origins and essence – nature-earth, and these were founded on sensing, feeling, seeing (as in vision), and being (as in experience). Do I repeat myself? For our purpose here, our gains have been in religion; our losses have been in spirituality. This requires a slow pace, cyclical time and deep awareness. [Spiritual Reality]

And if in reading *Sumer Is Icumen In,* we can re-learn *how-to survive (and enjoy) the mid-summer festival* and understand how we can integrate contemporary celebrations with our ancestral observances in order to preserve another fragment of our cultural heritage, then our feet will be on the right path. The Western view claims religions that were primal, natural and spiritual, evolved into monotheism but Dr Killingsworth thinks this is questionable. This Universal Oneness – the all-encompassing feeling that everything is interconnected and unified may be ours to experience if we are ever fortunate enough to be at say, Newgrange, and watch the narrow beam of the Summer Solstice sun travelling along the passage until it gradually illuminates the entire chamber at this sacred, cyclical time as it's done for thousands of years.

The experience is beyond words, analysis, conceptualization, theory, and reduction and fragmentation of the whole into parts and pieces to be defined, described and analysed. The mystical experience, cyclical time, timelessness, and inner being-perceptual enlightenment are not usually an integral part of book religion but came down from earlier times and other oriented ways of being which are not specifically religions in terms of deities and supernatural beliefs but may be connected with the biological-atmospheric spirituality of being. [Dr Jerry Killingsworth]

A Solitary Affair

It may be, of course, through choice or circumstances that we spend the Summer Solstice alone but this is no reason to miss out on the celebrations. It's the perfect day to prepare a special lunch or afternoon tea to eat al fresco with a small bottle of chilled prosecco to mark the turning of the year.

For this very special day of the year, we make sure we're up early to watch the sun rise even if we can't actually see the horizon, we can watch the rays from the rising sun spread across the land or city-scape ... reflecting in the windows of high-rise buildings and the amazing cloud formations in the city ... or casting light and shadow across rural farmland ... while we drink our first cup of tea or coffee of the morning. It's a very special time of the year and the reason why so many feel the need to make that pilgrimage to Stonehenge or Tara to experience the moment with like-minded people.

Personally speaking, I feel that if we can't observe the solstices and equinoxes at the *precise time* on that *exact day* then we don't need to bother at all because if we miss it, we're out of celestial synch anyway! The Summer Solstice, also known as aestival (of, or relating to the summer) solstice, occurs when one of the Earth's poles has its maximum tilt toward the Sun and marks the start of summer in the northern half of the globe.

After the solstice, the Sun appears to reverse course and head back in the opposite direction. The motion referred to here is the apparent path of the Sun when one views its position in the sky at the same time each day, for example, at local noon. Over the year, its path forms a sort of flattened figure eight, called an analemma. Of course, the Sun itself is not moving (unless you consider its own orbit around the Milky Way galaxy); instead, this change in position in the sky that we on Earth notice is caused by the tilt of Earth's axis as it orbits the Sun, as well as Earth's elliptical, rather than circular, orbit. [*The Old Farmer's Almanac*]

What is the exact time of the summer solstice?

- Bottom line: While the *solstice* is at the *exact* same *time* everywhere on Earth, it does depend on your clock and *time* zone.

- It will happen at 21:43 UTC (Universal Coordinated Time) on Saturday, June 20. If we're in the Eastern Time Zone of the United States, that's 5:43 p.m. June 20.

- But if you happen to live in Tokyo, for instance, our precise Summer Solstice moment actually happens at 6:43 a.m. on Sunday, June 21.

- In fact, all of Asia will observe the Solstice on June 21. Berlin, Germany, in Central Europe barely falls on the June 20 date at 11:43 p.m. local time. [EarthSky.org]

If we're going to engage in a solitary observance, we need to make sure the Solstice has actually happened and that we're doing on the right date! Perhaps we're going to treat ourselves to that special lunch or afternoon tea while the sun's still in the sky; perhaps we have a special, magical spot where we like to still and watch the world go by with a picnic arranged especially for the occasion. It may mean that we don't move out of the garden and serve ourselves on our best china while we enjoy a stay-at-home treat listening to the latest Blake album!

For the members of our Coven it is the time to renew the magical protections of our home and family – religiously at the solstices and equinoxes throughout the year – according to our own individual ways and means. And, as lavender is a fragrance of summer, what better preparation that an infusion of lavender water to spray around the house as part of our purification-protection rite. The 'straw', completely freed from the flowers, if burnt for incense the stalks diffuse a powerful, but agreeable odour.

For the Coven it is also time for a personal Tarot reading to see what's in store for us individually between today and the

Autumn Equinox. Although the solstice is often thought of as a day-long event, it does, in fact, represent a single moment in time: when the sun is at northernmost point from the earth's equator during a single year. In the UK in 2021, for example, the Summer Solstice takes place on 21st June at Stonehenge in Salisbury will feel the day's first rays at 04:52 and bid them farewell at 21:26: Hill of Tara sunrise will be 5.00 until sunset at 21.52. Synchronise your reading and if you draw 'the Sun' card all will be good ...

However, we choose to celebrate the Summer Solstice, we are calling upon the belief in our Ancestors in order to channel the energies to empower our own particular pagan tradition and, in doing so, we are empowering ourselves. By re-establishing a link with those who created some of the world's greatest 'sun' temples we are paying homage to our illustrious pagan past for which many of us might have lost the deep awareness. Here, we can, hopefully, reconnect to the cycles of the seasons that are an integral facet of ancient beliefs, rituals and an organic intelligence that allows us to read the open book of Nature.

Nevertheless, the 'wheel of the year' is an annual cycle of seasonal festivals, observed by many modern pagans, consisting of the year's chief solar events (solstices and equinoxes) and the midpoints between them. While names for each festival vary among diverse pagan traditions, syncretic treatments often refer to the four solar events as 'quarter days', particularly in Wicca. Differing sects of modern paganism also vary regarding the precise timing of each celebration, based on distinctions such as lunar phase and geographic hemisphere. Contemporary pagan festivals that rely on the 'wheel' are based to varying degrees on folk traditions, regardless of actual historical pagan practices.

In many traditions of modern pagan cosmology, all things are considered to be cyclical, with time as a perpetual cycle of growth and retreat tied to the Sun's annual death and rebirth. In Wicca-

influenced traditions, the festivals, being tied to solar movements, have generally been steeped in solar mythology and symbolism, centered on the life cycles of the sun. Similarly, the Wiccan esbats are traditionally tied to the lunar cycles. Together, they represent the most common celebrations in neo-paganism. [The Modern Magical Revival: Esbats and Sabbats]

As a result of all this inter-faith confusion, the traditional Summer Solstice had almost faded into oblivion due to being absorbed into the church calendar, re-dated and re-named to appease developing customs but, by re-energizing it as part of an authentic pagan tradition we are dragging it kicking and screaming, dancing, drumming, chanting and laughing into the 21st century.

Chapter Four

Koldt Bord

Since it is our northern cousins who have kept their own brand of Summer Solstice celebrations flourishing with more than a little enthusiasm, perhaps we should look towards Scandinavia and create a buffet-style table with salads, sandwiches, and drinks. That way, we won't need to worry about everyone finishing eating at the same time. There is literally nothing more Scandinavian than a good, old-fashioned s*mörgåsbord* – a type of meal, originating in Sweden, served buffet-style with multiple hot and cold dishes of various foods on a table and it's all about food and a great way of guzzling through a nice, big, wonderful luncheon. Except, *smorgasbord* is a Swedish word and in Norway and Denmark, it's called something else – *Koldt Bord* – cold table, or similar – with a few regional variations. But, as long as there is enough food to go round, people will be happy.

The word comes from the Swedish word *smörgås*, meaning 'open sandwich' or 'buttered bread', and bord, meaning 'table' – which is basically a buffet made up of many smaller dishes: 'a laid-out table'. The term first cropped up outside Scandinavia during the 1939 World's Fair in New York, when a Swedish restaurant served a *smorgasbord* as we know it today. This, however, was not the first occasion as this was more of an accidental invention. Many centuries earlier, people in well to-do homes had what was known as an 'Aquavit Table'. They would return back from whatever they had been doing (hunting moose or looking after their estates, etc.) and enjoy a few snacks. A few hours prior to dinner, shots of aquavit were served, likely as an afternoon pick-me-up. These were accompanied by a selection of cheeses, pickles and meats laid out on a side-table to snack on before the main meal. Over the years, the choice of dishes expanded and, one day, the Aquavit Table became the main event instead of the actual luncheon or dinner. Clever marketing people at the World Fair coined a new word that since then has been adopted into a word that works in many languages.

The essence of a real *smorgasbord* is all about taking our time to eat and talk with our guests as the Swedes do it – and share food, conversation and time. There is lots of food, granted, but the Scandis spend many hours eating it. No *smorgasbord* ever took an hour – and there is no time limit on how long they might sit there – the Danish Christmas Table, for example, can easily take an entire afternoon and end with an early dinner and most certainly result in quite a hangover, too. This is why these are usually done during high seasons such as Christmas, Easter and Midsummer when people plan big get-togethers and have time to relax and enjoy both food and company to the max. A real pagan extravaganza if ever there was one!

Traditionally, you start with herring and cheese, then dabble in seafood, gravlax, crawfish, shrimp and fish paté. The third round is cold cuts, ham, sausage, paté, salad and pickles and the fourth is warm dishes, meatballs and Jansson's Temptation – a potato casserole with cured sprats (a forage-fish like herring). A *smorgasbord* is usually served in 'rounds' – on a Swedish one, usually everything is set out at the start of the meal in buffet style, whereas in Denmark, each round is brought to the table one after the other in strict order and shared round.

Admittedly, it's tricky to know how to find our way around *smorgasbord etiquette* if we are a beginner, especially if we are in Denmark and nobody has told us that there are seven more *rounds* of food to follow the one we are eating. And what foods go together? Can we put remoulade on liver pate (answer: No!) *Rémoulade* is a European cold sauce based on mayonnaise. Although similar to tartar sauce, it is often more yellowish, sometimes flavored with curry, and often contains chopped pickles or piccalilli. It can also contain horseradish, paprika, anchovies, capers and a host of other items.

And do you ever put herring with prawns (Answer: NEVER). How much aquavit are you allowed to drink? (Answer: As much as you can, but not so much so that you appear drunk until everyone else is). Beginners will fill a plate like they are at an all-you-can-eat buffet. They will also hit the aquavit hard – and we just know that no novice will last till the end. Many a beginner has fallen off the *smorgasbord* wagon at round two in the morning and missed the party! The dishes on a Scandinavian *smorgasbord* vary seasonally and regionally, but the main dishes are the same – and these are also what connects Scandis together, despite living in a place three and a half times the size of Britain and with quite a varied food culture. This is where you will always find herring and meatballs!

One of our witch acquaintances adopted the idea of Scandi open-sandwiches following repeated holidays via continental ferries and business connections in Norway in the 1990s. *In Hearth & Garden: A Witch's Treasury*, Gabrielle Sidonie suggested that instead of preparing the open sandwiches in advance, leave the ingredients so that people can make up their own. Make up a selection to hand around and give people the idea and then invite them to help themselves. The foundation for these is a selection of thinly sliced breads on which a variety of meats, cheeses and salads can be attractively arranged. Do not overload the sandwiches or your guests will be landing up with their lunch/supper in their lap!

A simple, basic selection will do for starters which can be expanded as we become more ambitious at replacing them with genuine Scandi recipes:

Breads: brown, white, toasted, rolls, rye, French or Vienna
Selection of sliced cold meats
Slices of cold chicken or turkey
Paté

Shrimps, prawns or crab
Smoked salmon and pickled herring
Sliced, hard-boiled eggs
Assorted cheeses
Salad in separate dishes
Assorted pickles, gherkins and stuffed olives

A Midsummer festival isn't a true celebration without plenty of delicious food to indulge in. So, we've rounded up some favorite summer recipes to add to your Summer Solstice spread from *Umgas* Magazine that celebrates Swedish life and culture in the United States, to get us started:

What to Eat

Make a *smörgåsbord* buffet or a picnic since both will contain the same sort of foods. We have added some ** things that are essential – the other bits are fillers, so add as many as you fancy or have time to do. There are lots of different recipes for each dish on-line – some with different variations – so get cooking:

- Pickled herring** Arrange in bowls, decorate with onions rings on top and dill sprigs. A traditional way of preserving herring as food by pickling or curing. It is first cured with salt to extract water; then the salt is removed and the herring is brined in a vinegar, salt, and sugar solution, often with peppercorn, bay leaves, raw onions, and so on. Additional flavourings include sherry, mustard and dill, while other non-traditional ingredients have also begun being included in recent years. In the Nordic countries, depending on which of the dozens of herring flavourings are selected, it is eaten with dark rye bread, crisp bread, sour cream, or potatoes. This dish is common at Christmas, Easter and Midsummer, where it is frequently accompanied by spirits like akvavit.

- Gubbröra – boiled egg with pickled sprats. Eat with crispbread. *Gubbröra* means 'old man's mix', possibly because old men particularly like it! The mix is simply hard-boiled eggs, spiced-cured *ansjovis*, herbs and something to bind the mixture together. (Although *ansjovis* sounds like anchovies, they are actually sprats, but sometimes they are referred to as Swedish anchovies.)
- Classic *gubbröra* uses raw egg yolk as the binding but in this recipe, based on a version by Per Morberg a famous Swedish actor and TV chef, *gräddfil* (similar to soured cream) and crème fraiche are used instead. *Ansjovis* are quite different to Mediterranean anchovies, so you really do need to find the Swedish version! They are normally available from specialist stores and online.
- Gravad Lax cured salmon ** (goes well with rye bread). Gravlax or graved salmon is a Nordic dish consisting of salmon that is cured using salt, sugar, and dill. Gravlax is usually served as an appetizer, sliced thinly and accompanied by *hovmästarsås*, a dill and mustard sauce, either on bread or with boiled potatoes.
- Västerbotten Quiche – a delicious Swedish cheese pie, perfect eaten cold. Top with caviar sauce – red lumpfish roe mixed with a few large spoonsful of crème fraiche or sour cream.
- A great side dish for crayfish – this traditional cheese tart is often served with caviar dressing. Cheddar can be substituted for *Västerbotten*, which is a sharp Swedish cheese.
- New potatoes ** – Cook and allow to cool down, dress with melted butter and fresh dill. Serve them, with a bowl of what Swedes call *gräddfill* on the side – it's similar to crème fraiche – but lighter. You can get the exact same thing by mixing half natural yoghurt and half crème

fraiche. Add lots of chopped chives with the *gräddfill*, too – essential.

- Swedish Meatballs**. Well, you didn't think you could avoid meatballs, did you? You can easily find a recipe on how to make your own. Budget 2-3 meatballs per person for these, or if you use the smaller supermarket variety, budget about 3-4 per person.
- Beetroot Salad** It wouldn't be Midsummer without a good beetroot salad. Pickled beets and sweet apples come together in this traditional dish. Despite its bright pink color, this is a savoury salad with a simple sour cream and mayo binder, often served, along with meat-balls, red cabbage and apples.
- Extra salads – if you fancy making a more elaborate spread and trying something different.
- Beetroot Tart is a fab veggie option that both tastes and looks stunning. This tart works well served both warm and cold, and is lighter than traditional quiches as it uses less dairy filling. If you want a creamier filling, add a bit more crème fraiche or even some cream. [*Scandikitchen*]
- Bread ** Make a bread basket of lovely crisp-bread, rye bread and crusty bread so there is something for everyone.
- Cheeses – if you want to add a cheese selection.
- Dessert *must* incorporate strawberries** – that's the law. The more strawberries the better.
- If you want to know what Swedish summer tastes like, look no further than Swedish strawberry cake. For many Swedes, this cake is essential to midsummer and birthday celebrations. Every year, in the days leading up to midsummer, the cost of strawberries tends to skyrocket in Sweden. This is because Swedes have to eat strawberries or, more specifically, strawberry cake on midsummer's eve – no matter what the cost. An authentic Swedish strawberry cake is as simple as it is spectacular. It is essentially a

regular sponge cake filled with vanilla cream on the first layer, strawberry jam on the second and then smothered in whipped cream and strawberries. Once finished, the strawberry cake is a sight to behold in all its red and white glory – colourful, decadent, and absolutely mouth-wateringly delicious. An easier option of strawberries and cream also works!

What to drink

- Aquavit is needed for a traditional Scandi Midsummer. Serve slightly chilled in shot glasses. Be warned, it gets you drunk from the waist down.
- Also, serve nice beers and wine, if preferred, but this is less traditional (and doesn't work so well with aquavit, so do be careful of who you're playing footsie with under the table).
- A nice non-alcoholic drink is Elderflower or Lingonberry Cordial – great with both still and sparkling water.

How to arrange the table and buffet if you're having the party at home:

If arranging on a separate buffet table (recommended for 10 people or more), always arrange the fish at one end, starting with the herring, followed by any other fish dishes. Follow it with cold meats, then warm meats, side dishes and finally bread and butter. Cheese can be placed by the bread section or served separately at the end as a cheese board. Dessert is not usually brought out until the main *smörgåsbord* has been eaten down to the wooden table ... [Umgas Magazine]

As we can see, Summer Solstice celebrations are firmly entrenched as a Scandinavian custom and as they appear to have the whole thing taped, we can't go far wrong in emulating them. Our take on 'surviving' the Mid-Summer Festival is acknowledging the fact that this is an extremely hedonistic affair and one where everyone is encouraged to over-eat and drink in a true pagan fashion. And, who knows, we might even enjoy ourselves, too!

PS: Note to self: Stock up with plenty of bicarb in the bathroom and kitchen.

Chapter Five

The Celtic Twilight

The Celtic Revival (also referred to as the Celtic Twilight) was a variety of movements and trends in the 19th and 20th centuries that saw a renewed interest in all aspects of Celtic culture.

Research into the Gaelic and Brittonic cultures and histories of Britain and Ireland gathered pace from the late 17th century, by antiquaries and historians like Owen Jones in Wales and Charles O'Connor in Ireland. The key surviving manuscript sources were gradually located, edited and translated, monuments identified and published, and other essential groundwork in recording stories, music and language carried out. The Welsh antiquarian and author Iolo Morganwg fed the growing fascination in all things Brittonic by founding the Gorsedd, which would in turn spark the neo-druidism movement.

The Continental Celtic language is the now-extinct group of Celtic tongues that were spoken on the continent of Europe and in central Anatolia, as distinguished from the Insular Celtic languages of the British Isles, and Brittany. The term is mostly used in reference to the peoples of the British Iron Age prior to the Roman conquest, and their contemporaries in Ireland. At some point these languages split into the two major groups, Goidelic in Ireland and Brittonic in Great Britain, corresponding to the population groups of the Goidels (Gaels) on one hand and the Britons and the Picts on the other.

It is thought that by about the 6th century BC most of the inhabitants of the isles of Ireland and Britain were speaking Celtic languages. It is not entirely clear, however, if there was ever a 'Common Insular Celtic' language, the alternative being that the Celtic settlement of Ireland and Great Britain was undertaken by separate populations speaking separate Celtic dialects from the beginning. This would point to a single wave of immigration of early Celts, which divided into two isolated groups soon after their arrival, placing the split of Insular Celtic into Goidelic and Brythonic close to 500 BC. In an alternative scenario, the migration could have brought early Celts first to Britain (where a largely undifferentiated Insular Celtic was spoken initially), from whence Ireland was colonised only later. British and Goidelic were still essentially identical as late as the mid-1st century AD since there is no archaeological evidence pointing to a Celtic presence in Ireland prior to about 100BC.

The Goidelic branch would develop into Primitive Irish, Old Irish and Middle Irish, and only with the historical (medieval) expansion of the Gaels would it split into the modern Gaelic languages (Modern Irish, Scottish Gaelic, Manx). Common Brythonic, on the other hand, split into two branches, British and Pritenic as a consequence of the Roman invasion of Britain in the 1st century. By the 8th century, Pritenic had developed into Pictish (which would be extinct during the 9th century or so), while British had split into Old Welsh and Old Cornish. Cumbric (Old English: *Cumbrisċ*) was a variety of the Common Brittonic language deriving either from Brittonic (Welsh *craig*) or *Goidelic* (Scottish *Gaelic creag*).

The Welsh language (or *y Gymraeg*), however, has been spoken continuously in Wales throughout recorded history, and in recent centuries has been easily the most widely spoken of all the Celtic languages. But by 1911 it had become a minority language, spoken by only 43.5% of the population. While this decline continued over the following decades, the language did not die out and by the start of the 21st century, numbers began to increase once more. Historically, large numbers of Welsh people spoke only Welsh. Over the course of the 20th century this monolingual population had 'all but disappeared', but a small percentage remained at the time of the 1981 census.

Among the Insular Celts, the year was divided into a light

half (summer) and a dark half (winter). As the day was seen as beginning at sunset, so the year was seen as beginning with the arrival of the darkness, at *Calan Gaeaf / Samhain* (around 1st November in the modern calendar). The light half of the year started at *Calan Haf / Beltaine* (around 1st May, modern calendar). This observance of festivals beginning the evening before the festival day is still seen in the celebrations and folkloric practices among the Gaels, such as the traditions of *Oíche Shamhna* (Samhain Eve) among the Irish and *Oidhche Shamhna* among the Scots.

Calan Mai 'Calend (first day) of May' or *Calan Haf* 'Calend of Summer' is a May Day holiday of Wales held on 1st May. Celebrations start on the evening before, known as May Eve with the traditional lighting of bonfires celebrating this occasion happening annually in South Wales until the middle of the 19th century.

Customs

- On *Nos Galan Mai* or May Eve, villagers gather hawthorn (Welsh: *draenen wen*, 'white-thorn') branches and flowers which they would then use to decorate the outside of their houses, celebrating new growth and fertility.
- In Anglesey and Caernarfonshire it would be common on May Eve to have *gware gwr gwyllt* 'playing straw man' or *crogi gwr gwellt* 'hanging a straw man'. A man who had lost his sweetheart to another, would make a man out of straw and put it somewhere in the vicinity of where the girl lived. The straw man represented her new sweetheart and had a note pinned to it. Often the situation led to a fight between the two men at the May Fair.
- Being the time between Summer and Winter, *Calan Haf* would be the time to stage a mock fight between the two seasons. The man representing Winter carried a stick of blackthorn (Welsh: *draenen ddu* 'black-thorn') and a shield

that had pieces of wool stuck on it to represent snow. The man representing Summer was decorated with garlands of flowers and ribbons and carried a willow-wand which had spring flowers tied on it with ribbons. A mock battle took place in which the forces of Winter threw straw and dry underbrush at the forces of Summer who retaliated with birch branches, willow (Welsh: *helygen*) rods, and young ferns (Welsh: *rhedyn*). Eventually the forces of Summer would win and a May King and Queen were chosen and crowned, after which there was feasting, dancing, games and drinking until the next morning.

- May Day was the time that the *twmpath chwarae* or 'tump for playing' (a kind of village green) was officially opened. Through the summer months in some villages the people would gather on the *twmpath chwarae* in the evenings to dance and play various sports. The green was usually situated on the top of a hill and a mound was made where the fiddler or harpist sat. Sometimes branches of oak decorated the mound and the people would dance in a circle around it.

- *Dawnsio haf* 'summer dancing' was a feature of the May Day celebration, as was *carolau Mai* 'May carols' also known as *carolau haf* 'summer carols' or *canu dan y pared* 'singing under the wall', these songs often being of a bawdy or sexual nature. The singers would visit families on May morning accompanied by a harpist or fiddler, to wish them the greetings of the season and give thanks to 'the bountiful giver of all good gifts'. If their singing was thought worthy, they would be rewarded with food, drink, and possibly money.

- Common drinks during *Calan Mai* festivities were *metheglin* or mead. Sometimes it was made of herbs, including woodruff, a sweet-smelling herb which was often put in wine in times past to make a man merry and act as a tonic for the heart and liver. Elderberry and rhubarb wines were popular and the men also liked various beers. *[Welsh Customs for Calan Haf]*

Lá Bealtaine is the festival marking the beginning of summer and celebrated by the Irish Celts on May Day. They would perform various rituals, hold feasts, and light fires to celebrate birth and fertility. Bealtaine (or Belltaine) appears in a 9/10th-century Irish glossary apparently written by the King of Munster/Bishop of Cashel, Cormac úa Cuilennáin. Beltane marks the beginning of Summer occurring half-way between the Spring Equinox and the Summer Solstice.

Customs

- Cormac's glossary was translated in the 19th century by John O'Donovan who wrote: BELLTAINE 'May-day' i.e. bil-tene i.e. lucky fire, i.e. two fires which Druids used to make with great incantations, and they used to bring the cattle [as a safeguard] against the diseases of each year to those fires [in marg.] they used to drive the cattle between them.

- Comparing the two we can see the original text never contained 'May-Day' and it was added by O'Donovan as part of the translation. A footnote added by the editor refers to an eleventh century Psalter called the *Southampton Psalter*, Insular illuminated Psalter from Ireland.

- In the Ulster Cycle of Irish mythology Bealtaine is mentioned in the tale Tochmarc Emire ('The Wooing of Emer') recorded in *Lebor na hUidre* (the Book of the Dun Cow), compiled approximately 1050 A.D. It is believed this story may have been first written down by Irish monks in the 6th century to preserve national literature but most collections had been destroyed by invading Vikings.

- In 'The Wooing of Emer', it states: Bend Suain, son of Rosc Mele, which she said this is the same thing, viz., that I shall fight without harm to myself from Samuin, i.e., the end of summer. For two divisions were formerly on the year, viz., summer from Beltaine (the first of May), and winter from Samuin to Beltaine.

The bonfires of *Bealtaine.*

- *Foras Feasa ar Éirinn* ('The History of Ireland') written by Geoffrey Keating, a 17th-century historian, mentions the Convention of Uisneach held at Bealltaine. The men of Ireland would hold meetings to exchange goods and valuables. However, they also offer sacrifices to the chief god called Beil. They would light two fires in every district in Ireland in honor of him when they would then drive the weaklings of each species of cattle between the fires to shield them from all diseases during the year. Uisneach, or the hill of Uisneach, is in Co. Westmeath. It's an ancient ceremonial site and the symbolic center of the land in Irish mythology.

- Located beside the town of Raphoe in Co Donegal is Beltany Stone Circle, dating from the late Bronze Age period. The Circle has a diameter of 145 feet and made up of 64 large standing stones enclosing a low earth platform. On the north-east side, one of the stones is decorated with cup-marks facing into the inner circle. This stone, the only decorated stone in the circle, aligns with the sunrise during Bealtaine and a stone head found within the circle was carved between 400BC–400AD indicating the monument was in use for centuries.

- Many people today follow Bealtaine celebrations with the Bealtaine Fire at Uisneac being lit each year.

- In pastoral life it is traditionally the time when livestock held at the farmstead since last Samhain are driven back to the summer pastures. A tradition that some farmers still uphold today.

- Beltaine is a festival of life. The fertility that was dramatically rising at the Spring Equinox now reaches its peak. The potential becomes conception and manifests itself in the abundant growth all around.

- The crowning of a 'May Queen and King' and the tradition of dancing around a 'Maypole' are May-day celebrations symbolic of fertility.

- Beltaine along with Samhain are the two biggest fire festivals of the year.

Grian-stad samhraidh is Scottish Gaelic for the Summer Solstice – the moment when the hemisphere is most inclined toward the sun. Here are some of the traditional ways in which Scotland has celebrated the longest day of the year.

Customs

- Midsummer, the point that marks the turning of the year as the days begin to shorten is the source of many kinds of ritual and celebration all over Scotland. The festival itself is primarily a Celtic fire festival traditionally celebrated on either the 23rd or 24th of June, although the longest day actually falls on the 21st. Its importance to our ancestors is evident in the large number of stone circles and other ancient monuments are aligned to the sunrise on this day.

- Midsummer fires were still a common phenomenon well into the 18th century, especially in rural areas where traditional beliefs could co-exist with Christianity seemingly without conflict. After Christianity became widely adopted in Britain, the festival became known as St John's day and was still celebrated as an important day, but in many parts of the country the old ways would still be clung to.

- Although the exact customs varied there was a common theme – that of blessing the crops and beasts of the land with fire, generally by walking them around the fire in a sun-wise direction. It was also customary for people to jump high through the flames, folklore suggesting that the height reached by the most athletic jumper, would be the height of that year's harvest.

- Celebrations began on the evening of the Feast of St John the Baptist (June 24th), and the main focal point of the festivities was the bonfire, although the accompanying rites were more solemnly observed in the north than in the Lowlands, where the emphasis was on fun and festiveness. These were generally lit after sunset – which at this time of year would have been very late indeed and around the fire there was food and drink to be had, along with dancing (actively discouraged by the church).

- In some bonfires a bone was thrown or ritually placed into it, symbolic of the animal that would previously have been sacrificed to appease the sun god. Branches of birch were collected and hung over the doorways for protection, and torches of heather were lit from the main fire and taken back to the homestead by the head of the house, where he would then go round the field sun-wise, three times to bless the crops and ensure a good harvest. The same was done around the byre to bless the cattle and safeguard them against disease. Meanwhile, the young men and boys remained at the bonfire, where they waited for the flames to die down before leaping them and then heading home at sunrise.

- Orkney is one of the places that clung to the old traditions the longest with Johnsmas celebrations a common practice until the mid-19th century. Here the peats for the fire were provided by those whose horses had suffered disease, or been gelded, during the year, with the livestock then being led sun-wise around the flames. Blazing heather was carried into byres and, where possible, among the cattle to help ensure procreation. In the preceding century, people were also in the habit of circling their houses and fields with blazing torches.

Common Riding Festivals: In many Lowland areas the 'Common Riding' Festivals incorporated many of the same aspects and customs, and are also staggered throughout summer. Part of the Summer Solstice ritual was to walk the sacred paths, reinforcing boundaries both spiritual and physical. 'Riding the Bounds' forms an important part of Common Riding customs to this day and forms the centre-piece of the Peebles Beltane festival.

- The Eve of St. John has special magical significance and was used by Sir Walter Scott as the title, and theme, for one of his poems. He invented a legend in which the lady of Smailholm Tower, near Kelso, keeps vigil by the midnight fires three nights in a row and is visited by her lover. When her husband returns from battle, she learns he slew that lover on the first night, and she has been entertained by a very physical ghost!
- Traditionally, this Summer Solstice period fell between the planting and harvesting of crops, leaving people who worked the land time to relax. This is why June became the traditional month for weddings. The first (or only) full moon in June was called the 'honey moon' because many believed it was the best time to take honey from beehives.
- Herbs and flowers were also traditionally gathered on this day and often placed under a pillow in the hope of important dreams, especially dreams about future lovers. Love was a common theme in midsummer festivals with

paired sweethearts leaping over bonfires hand in hand or throwing flowers across the flames to each other. In one somewhat convoluted (or maybe desperate) ritual, girls could take home a partly burned peat from the midsummer fire, extinguish it in a tub of urine, place it above the door lintel and wait till next morning. When the peat was then broken open, a fibre would show the hair colour of the girl's future husband.

- St John's Eve was seen as a time when the veil between this world and the next was thin, and when powerful forces were abroad. Vigils were often held during the night and it was said that if you spent a night at a sacred site during Midsummer Eve, you would gain the powers of a bard, on the down side you could also end up utterly mad, dead, or be spirited away by the fairies. *Uamh Tom a' Mhor*, a 40-yard-long cave on the slopes of Schiehallion, the geographical centre of Scotland has been positively identified by some as the actual entrance to Otherworld. Those venturing into it to join the annual fairy shindig on midsummer's evening may find themselves staying longer than they bargained for with local legends telling of unlucky travellers being waylaid for up to 30 years.

- For many the most identifiable midsummer image is that of neo-pagans and standing stones, but it is worth remembering that every generation has its own beliefs and customs, some die out forever, some are revived and adapted for the modern world and some never leave us. Midsummer bonfires are somehow elemental, a reminder of our pagan past and an important way of remembering the superstitious days when survival was dependent on good harvests and healthy cattle.

While at the pole, there is continuous daylight around the Summer Solstice, in Scotland they also experience very long days, being situated in the north of Europe. On 21st June 2018, sunrise in Shetland, for example – the most northerly point in Scotland – took place at 03.38 and the sun set at 22.34, meaning the longest day of the year was 18 hours, 55 minutes and 30 seconds long. Depending on the calendar, the Summer Solstice takes place any time between 20th and 22nd -traditionally being an important time in Scotland and other northern countries, and is still celebrated as the longest day of the year after the dark months of winter.

While in England, people flock to the sacred site of Stonehenge, in Scotland they have their own traditions and spiritually historic sites to visit. Most of the history of Solstice celebrations can be found in Orkney and Shetland, since there's a strong influence from Scandinavia where Summer Solstice remains an important celebration. Similar to the Beltaine festivals of 1st May, which were celebrated in ancient Scotland and Ireland, Summer Solstice sees the use of torches and fire as a symbol of light defeating darkness.

Marking the midway point of the harvest season, many of the Solstice celebrations revolved around warding off evil spirits and bringing good fortune. People would walk around their homes, fields and towns wielding torches to banish evil spirits, while protective plants such as St John's Wort would be draped over doors or stashed under pillows to bring good luck. The fern is also linked to good luck and according to mythology, it blooms for a short time on the eve of Midsummer, bringing good fortune to those that find it. Eating elderberries was also thought to protect against witchcraft, as the elderflower plant peaks around Summer Solstice. Some creatures are also thought to have curative qualities at this time of year, such as snakes and frogs.

- But if there's nothing planned, do as some people do and try climbing a local hill to take in the sunset and do some star-gazing?

Until relatively recently the Gaelic Scots tended not to refer to the months and days of the year, but instead marked the time according to how many days before or after a certain season or festival the event they were referring to was. These seasons and festivals were an integral part of the social calendar, and were important in marking the cycle of the agricultural and fishing calendar as well, and at their core these festivals have their roots in pre-Christian Ireland.

The Gaelic year can be broken up into four quarters, with each quarter starting at the beginning of a new season. These are *earrach* (spring), *samhradh* (summer), *fogharadh* (autumn), and *geamhradh* (winter). Given the close historical ties between Ireland, Scotland, and Man, it's inevitable that early Irish sources are an important source for our understanding of these origins and many of the traditions that are associated with them. Early Irish myth clearly divides the year in the same way, and this can be seen most explicitly in the tale 'The Wooing of Emer' where the year is split up into:

> *In Scottish lore, the sources for which tend to be later than much of the historical sources available from Ireland, evidence of this sort of divide also exists. The winter months were often referred to as the period of the 'little sun', or else they were called na tri miosa marbh (the three dead months), an raithe marbh (the dead quarter) or else raithe marbh na bliadhna (the dead quarter of the year). The time between Bealltaine to Samhain was known as the 'big sun'. The Cailleach, known as 'the daughter of Grianan' (the 'little sun'), ruled over the winter months, keeping the weather harsh and cold. In some versions she transforms herself into a boulder as the time of the 'big sun' starts, or else she is transformed from an old hag into a beautiful maiden.*

Celebrating Midsummer

Manannán is a god found in both Irish and Scottish traditions (and, of course, Manx), who is quite a popular deity in modern polytheism where he is seen as an Otherworldly king and gatekeeper, a god of the sea and watery places, a god who tests and challenges. For many Gaelic polytheists he is the god most naturally associated with Midsummer celebrations, with feasts and rites being held in his honour. Áine also has a claim to the day, and traditionally has her stronghold at Cnoc Áine in County Limerick, where funerary rites were held in her honour on Midsummer's Eve.

According to a portion of *Acallamh na Seanórach*, Áine was married to Manannán after her brother fell in love with Manannán's wife, and Manannán fell in love with (or was seduced by) Áine, prompting a swap. In spite of their close relationship and the fact that they were both honoured in certain parts of the Gaelic world on the same day, there appear to be no suggestions that they were honoured together as a pair, by Gaelic polytheists who feel it is appropriate to do so. You could, if you wish, make some simple offerings to *An Trì Naomh* in general, and perhaps give a prayer to the Sun as you make your own observances.

- Bring in some birch and place above the doors for protective purposes.
- If possible, light a bonfire (with blessings being said) at sunset, as the focal point for your celebrations, tending to it until sunrise begins.
- Prepare a feast, making sure you have enough for offerings, too – bannocks, 'gudebread', lamb, fish (especially if you live near the sea), or a good quality bread soaked in spiced and sweetened milk are all traditional dishes.
- Sain the boundaries with a flaming torch, paying attention to anything you're growing for harvesting later.
- A visit to the beach or hillside is especially appropriate on this day, where offerings and prayers of thanks to Manannán and/or Áine should be made. For Manannán,

rushes are traditional (for 'paying the rents' to him), while meadow-sweet may be appreciated by Áine. Other offerings can be made, including seasonal fruit like berries, or baked goods containing them.

- Dances, games, general fun and festivities in Manannán's and/or Áine's honour.
- Around midnight, collect herbs for use throughout the year – St John's Wort, fern seeds, mugwort, yarrow, and elderberries are all particularly appropriate.

As a reconstructionist belief, Gaelic polytheism looks to scholarly, historical, and archaeological sources to help inform its worldview, beliefs and religious expression, along with heavy reference of historical folklore and surviving folk practices and traditions. As a polytheistic religion it honors many deities. Although the focus is on the gods of the Gaels – from what's now known as Ireland, Scotland, and the Isle of Man. As an animistic religion, Gaelic polytheism takes the view that pretty much everything has some kind of spirit or spiritual essence, be it a place, an object, or a living being.

As an ancestor-venerating religion, it also focuses on honoring the ancestors. The ancestors, together with the gods and spirits, might collectively be referred to as Na Trí Naomh or An Trì Naomh ("The Sacred Three" in Irish and Gaelic, respectively). Or else we might call them the dé ocus andé, or "gods and ungods," a phrase found in Old Irish, which seems to refer to the gods and… everything or everyone else who isn't divine but is still worthy of addressing. As an earth-honoring religion, Gaelic Polytheists view the land as sacred. This is partly because we see our gods as being a part of the landscape (although they are not just of the landscape) as much as we might encounter spirits of the land, and so we should do our part in co-existing in a way that's sensitive and respectful to this face. But it's also because the land around us has been shaped – for better

or worse – by our ancestors, who are also important to us. The land
around us has lessons for us to learn, and it is our responsibility to
care for, and to respect our environment – our sacred landscape –
because what we do to it will form a legacy for our descendants, too.
[gaelicpolytheism.wordpress.com]

Similarly, empathy with Celtic romanticism carved a deep furrow
in the burgeoning trend of modern paganism under the heading
of Celtic Reconstructionist Paganism (CR) as an approach to
Celtic neo-paganism, which emphasised historical accuracy over
eclecticism such as is found in many forms of neo-druidism and
contemporary paganism. In an effort to reconstruct and revive
the tradition in a Celtic cultural context, the movement originated
in discussions among amateur scholars and neo-pagans in the
mid-1980s, and evolved into an independent tradition by the
early 1990s.

As contemporary paganism grew in scope and popularity,
some Euro-Americans saw the pre-Christian beliefs of their
ancestors as being worthy of revival, and the study of mythology
and folklore as a way to accomplish this. While most neo-druid
groups of the period were primarily interested in 'revitalizing
the spirit of what they believe was the religious practice of
pre-Roman Britain', the Celtic Reconstructionists focused
on only 'reconstructing what can be known from the extant
historical record'. Many of those who eventually established
the reconstructionist movements were involved in modern
pagan groups during the 1970s and 1980s and much dialogue
in the 1980s took place at workshops and discussions at pagan
festivals and gatherings, as well as in the pages of current pagan
publications. With the emergence of the Internet in the late
1980s and early 1990s, many of these groups and individuals
came together online and thus began a period of increased
communication, and led to the growth of the movement.

The first appearance in print of the term 'Celtic Reconstructionist' used to describe a specific religious movement and not just a style of Celtic studies, was by Kym Lambert ní Dhoireann in the Spring, 1992 issue of *Harvest Magazine* – who credits Kathryn Price NicDhàna with originating the term. NicDhàna, however, credits her early use to a simple extrapolation of Margot Adler's use of 'pagan reconstructionists' in the original, 1979 edition of *Drawing Down the Moon*. Eventually, this pairing of terms became an accepted figure of speech and in the pagan/polytheist communities, *reconstructionist* now came to mean traditions that specifically *excluded* eclecticism.

Drawing Down the Moon: Witches, Druids, Goddess-Worshippers, and Other Pagans in America Today was a ground-breaking sociological study of contemporary paganism in the USA written by an American Wiccan journalist , described by the *N.Y Times* as 'a self-described Wiccan high priestess' in her obituary:

> *Ms. Adler was drawn to neo-paganism in the early '70s, she said, because its invocation of ancient goddesses appealed to her feminism and its ecological concerns resonated with her love of nature. In her sprawling apartment, on Central Park West, she maintained a pagan shrine in her bedroom and had formerly helped lead "a small coven" in the living room, The Times reported in 1991.*

According to *The New York Times*, the book 'is credited with both documenting new religious impulses and being a catalyst for the panoply of practices now in existence' and 'helped popularize earth-based religions'. Adler was 'a recognized witch' and according to the entry in *The Encyclopedia of Witches & Witchcraft*:

> *On a trip to England, Adler investigated the history of the Druids, and in the process discovered numerous Pagan organisations. She subscribed to The Waxing Moon which led her introduction to Witchcraft ... In the early 1970s, contemporary Witchcraft was rapidly gaining adherents in the US having been imported from*

England under the aegis of Raymond and Rosemary Buckland, followers of Gerald Gardner. The Craft was modified under numerous American covens and Adler joined a [Gardnerian] study group in Brooklyn by the name of New York Coven of Welsh Traditional Witches. Another group hived off from that coven to observe the Gardnerian tradition and Adler followed. She was initiated as a first-degree Gardnerian priestess in 1973.

The book views neo-paganism in the United States from a sociological standpoint, discussing the history and various forms of the movement's development. It contains excerpts from many interviews with average pagans, as well as with well-known leaders and organizers in the community. Originally, Margot Adler had intended to include Britain in her survey but – not surprisingly – British groups and individuals proved reluctant to participate. With the growth of the Internet during the 1990s, hundreds of individuals and groups gradually joined the discussions online and in print, and the movement became more of an umbrella group, with a number of recognized sub-traditions. Although it must be stated that Coven of the Scales and traditional British Old Craft in general, are neither reconstructionist or revivalist – having antecedents that are historically proven and tending to keep themselves 'socially distanced' from neo-paganism in general and American Wicca in particular.

While the indigenous Celtic religions were largely obliterated by Christianity, many traditions have survived in the form of folklore, mythology, songs, and prayers; while many folkloric practices never completely died out, and some reconstructionists claim to have survivals of Irish, Scottish or Welsh folkloric customs in their families of origin. Language study and preservation, and participation in other cultural activities such as Celtic music, dance and martial arts forms, are seen as a core part of the tradition. Participation in the living Celtic cultures –

the cultures that exist in the 'areas in which Celtic languages are actually spoken and in which Celtic traditions have been most faithfully handed down to the present day' – is a vital part of their cultural work and spiritual practice.

Like many other modern pagan traditions, Celtic Reconstructionism has no sacred texts and so personal research is encouraged. In order to more fully reconstruct pre-Christian Celtic beliefs, many Celtic Reconstructionists study archaeology, historical manuscripts, and comparative religion, primarily of Celtic cultures, but sometimes other European cultures, as well – especially from where large-scale migrations have taken place. Celtic Reconstructionists are not pan-Celtic in practice, but rather immerse themselves in a particular Celtic culture, such Gaelic, Welsh or Gaulish.

According to Kathryn Price NicDhàna, Celtic Reconstructionists believe that while it is helpful to study a wide variety of Celtic cultures as an aid to religious reconstruction, and to have a broader understanding of religion in general, in practice these cultures are not automatically lumped together. In addition to cultural preservation and scholarly research, Celtic Reconstructionists believe that mystical, ecstatic practices are a necessary balance to scholarship, and that this balance is a vital component of any Celtic Reconstructionist tradition.

As was demonstrated by the Office of Public Works live-streaming of the Solstice Sunrise event at Newgrange since the traditional gathering for both the Summer and Winter Solstices of 2020 at the Neolithic passage tomb were cancelled due to Covid-19 pandemics. However, the absence of visitors from this annual event at Newgrange presented a unique opportunity to carry out research which would not have been possible in any other year. In the preceding weeks, either side of the Solstice, the movement of the sunlight coming through the roof box into the passage and chamber will be scientifically measured and monitored, to determine how the beam of dawn light interplays with the chamber as we move towards Solstice and then past it.

Nevertheless, the OPW took advantage of the silence to make sure that people who wished to see the Solstice sun rise were able to experience this wonderful phenomenon live on-line from any location around the world.

While Celtic Reconstructionists strive to revive the religious practices of historical Celtic peoples as accurately as possible, they acknowledge that some aspects of their religious practice are reconstructions and that their practices are based on cultural survivals, augmented with the study of early Celtic beliefs found in texts and the work of scholars and archaeologists. Feedback from scholars and experienced practitioners is sought before a new practice is accepted as a valid part of a reconstructed tradition.

Like the Hill of Tara – a site that has been in use for more than 5000 years as a place of burial and assembly, it grew to fame as the legendary inauguration site of the ancient High Kings of Ireland. Once the ancient seat of power in Ireland – 142 kings are said to have reigned there in prehistoric and historic times – in ancient Irish religion and mythology Temair was the sacred place of dwelling for the gods, and the entrance to Otherworld. The skies above Ireland's iconic terrain can paint beautifully memorable pictures if caught at the right moment through a tradition that has lasted for thousands of years. Visitors and locals alike come together to appreciate the Summer and Winter Solstices, which are especially stunning when viewed from the ancient structures left behind by Ireland's Neolithic inhabitants, who often aligned their structures with these celestial events for mysterious reasons we still don't fully understand. Nevertheless, hundreds of people turn out each year to the Hill of Tara to celebrate the Summer Solstice in a tradition that dates back thousands of years.

The ancient Irish swore their oaths by the 'Three Realms' – of Land, Sea, and Sky and based on this precedent, reconstructed Gaelic ritual structures acknowledge the Land, Sea and Sky, with the Fire of inspiration as a central force that unites the realms. Many Celtic Reconstructionists maintain altars and shrines to their patron spirits and deities, often choosing to place them at outdoor, natural locations such as wells, streams, and special trees. Some practice divination: ogham is a favored method, as are folkloric customs such as the taking of omens from the shapes of clouds or the behavior of birds and animals.

NicDhàna and ní Dhoireann have stated that they coined the term 'Celtic Reconstructionist' specifically to distinguish their practices and beliefs from those of eclectic traditions like Wicca and Neo-druidism, since there has been some controversy around the use of the term 'Gaelic Traditionalists' by groups outside of the *Gaeltacht* and the *Gàidhealtachd* areas of Ireland, Scotland and Nova Scotia. As Kym Lambert ní Dhoireann put it: 'Gaelic Traditionalists' means those living and raised in the living cultures and [who] are keeping their culture, language and music alive, not any of the American polytheistic groups that have been using it lately. The Celtic Reconstructionists *FAQ* states that due to those in the Gaelic-speaking areas having a prior claim to the term, most Reconstructionists have been uncomfortable with the choice of other reconstructionists to call themselves 'Traditionalists'. [*The Green Triangle*]

There has been cross-pollination between many neo-pagan and reconstructionist groups, and although there is significant crossover of membership between various traditions, they have largely differing goals and methodologies in their approach to religious form. Reconstructionists tend to place high priority on historical authenticity and traditional practice. Others tend to prefer a modern eclectic approach, focusing on 'the spirit of what they believe was the religious practice of pre-Roman Britain'.

While modern Celtic paganism refers to any type of modern paganism or contemporary pagan movements based on the ancient Celtic religion; Celtic Wicca is a modern tradition of Wicca that incorporates some elements of Celtic mythology and employs the same basic theology, rituals and beliefs as most other forms of Wicca. Celtic Wiccans use the names of Celtic deities, mythological figures, and seasonal festivals within a Wiccan ritual structure and belief system, rather than a historically Celtic one. Many others, however, assume a pagan identity by joining the thousands of people who regularly attend the festivals organized at the ancient monuments without aligning themselves to any particular belief or tradition.

When we are talking about revivalist traditions within the pagan community, we have to be triply circumspect when we hazard a guess as to 'what was' and that which 'probably may have been'. This is a trap that has confounded many an academic who has pontificated upon the dubious 'intricacies' of traditional witchcraft without a clear understanding of what lies beneath the surface. Similarly, the contemporary- traditions (especially those with American roots) cannot speak for 'any non-Gardnerian, non-Alexandrian, non-Wiccan or pre-modern form of the Craft, especially if it has been inspired by historical forms of witchcraft and folk magic', as the late Michael Howard explained.

Witchcraft has fascinated some highly respected scholars in the past who have attracted derision from their peers for giving our remote ancestors more credit than was seen as their due for the sophisticated knowledge that comes with Craft learning. The likes of Reginald Scot (1584), Charles Leyland (1899), Margaret Murray (1921) and Tom Lethbridge (1962) did right by their subject in talking to those who actually practiced the Old Craft ... *but* ... without a total emersion in the Elder Faith, they were unable to fully understand and/or interpret the information they were being given. True witchcraft has always been notoriously obtuse – which is its strength and its saving grace – since this has protected it from infiltration since the gods' dog was a pup!

It's only by sifting through the dust to extract the nuggets of truth can we discover whether that core information came from authentic sources, or whether it was taken from the gossip of the time, *a la* William Shakespeare, Ben Jonson and Thomas Middleton! Any true witch must take a leaf of wisdom from the Japanese poet, Basho's book:

> *Go to the pine if you want to learn about the pine, or to the bamboo if you want to learn about the bamboo. And in doing so, you must leave your subjective preoccupation with yourself. Otherwise you impose yourself on the object and do not learn.*

Therefore, whilst it is perfectly acceptable to refer to the Summer Solstice as *Litha* if we belong to the Wiccan ... or an Anglo-Saxon revivalist tradition ... but it is not acceptable to impose this custom on other pagans, or attempt to correct them if they do not conform to our way of speaking. Neither is it pardonable to pass this erroneous information on to the next generation of pagans without any form of explanation. It is an indisputable *fact* that our ancient Ancestors looked upon the Summer Solstice as an important part of their belief and set this down in stone ... but the folklore and customs that have come down to us have been adulterated and mixed to such a degree that we are unable to identify them as having any authentic ancient origins.

We also have Antony Shaffer's fictional account of *The Wicker Man* to contend with (book and film) that takes place on the traditional Celtic start to summer – sunset on May Day – as the onlookers chant a powerful rendering of *Sumer Is Icumen In* to a sinister drumbeat. Stefan Gullatz's academic paper, *The Wicker Man, The Uncanny, and the Clash of Moral Cultures* concludes by observing:

> *Imagine what a lesser director from the Hammer Studios would have done to the film, if he had been commissioned to translate the script by Anthony Shaffer; how hard he would have found it to resist the temptation to attribute to the islanders a satanic evil.*

Nevertheless, here, we can discover new and exciting ways

of surviving (and enjoying) the truly pagan excesses of the Midsummer Festival. We can establish and instigate a new *smörgåsbord* of traditions of our own for the purpose of celebration and observance and, in time, they may even be integrated into future pagan revels but we should never lose sight of our own authentic history. It is impossible to impose a unilateral identity on all pagans and hope that they will conform, since the majority of those who crusade under the collective banner of paganism only pay lip-service to the Craft of Witches.

Because witches work with natural cyclic tides in their magical workings, it can be interesting when the powerful energies of the Summer Solstice coincide with increased solar activity! The Sun produces a solar wind – a continuous flow of charged particles – that can affect us on Earth. It can, for example, disrupt communications, navigation systems, and satellites; solar activity can also cause power outages, such as the extensive Canadian blackout in 1989.

Our planet Earth does not deserve more bad news. A global pandemic which continues to kill scores everyday to the ongoing threats caused by climate change - there is a lot on our plate. And now, there's more - The Sun has awoken just a couple of weeks before the Summer Solstice. A few days ago, millions of tonnes of super hot gas was ejected from the surface of Sun and shot off towards Earth. Officially known as a 'coronal mass ejection', the event wasn't powerful enough to cause serious harm to the planet. But it did set off the strongest geo-magnetic storm seen on our planet in years. Not many people even felt it. But scientists believe this points to a worrying trend in the future - that the Sun is up and running after years of dormancy just in time for this year's Summer Solstice and as we work out ways to harnessing this amazing energy! [IOWN]

This mid-year natural event is infused with mystery and wonder. And it's more than the effect of Shakespeare's faerie spectacle or

Woody Allen's comedy. We feel this ancient sense of delicious delight and mystery deserves to be celebrated in ways that make this longest day start to summer — or longest night winter kickoff, depending on where you live — even more of a dream says The Sleep Club:

The incredible meaning placed upon this magical time of year appears to come from what it signaled for ancient cultures. Without further ado, we present wondrous and magical ways to embrace your inner Druid, Witch, Faerie, and Wiccan and give into the dream of Summer Solstice. If you're looking for good traditional wreaths, they'll include summer flowers and herbs you can place on your head, your hearth, your door to welcome the longest day. The Northern Hemisphere's Summer Solstice is a celebration of folly and mystery. The dreams we dream leading up to and on that day feel more whimsical, somehow, as if the sun creating the longest day fills our nights with glowing, dewy visions of magic. However

If we shadows have offended,
Think but this, and all is mended,
That you have but slumber'd here
While these visions did appear.
And this weak and idle theme,
No more yielding but a dream,
Gentles, do not reprehend:
if you pardon, we will mend:
And, as I am an honest Puck,
If we have unearned luck
Now to 'scape the serpent's tongue,
We will make amends ere long;
Else the Puck a liar call;
So, good night unto you all.
Give me your hands, if we be friends,

And Robin shall restore amends.
– Robin "Puck" Goodfellow, *A Midsummer Night's Dream*

Sources & Bibliography

Taking a leaf out of Aleister Crowley's book, it is always a good move to go from each respected author to those that have been quoted in the text or bibliography:

> It established a rational consecution in my research; and as soon as I reached a certain point the curves became re-entrant, so that my knowledge acquired a comprehensiveness which could never have been so satisfactorily attained by any arbitrary curriculum. I began to understand the real relation of one subject to another ...

This technique often takes us to valuable out-of-print volumes that contain material not to be found repeated *ad nauseam* on the internet and this in turn, gives our own reading and writing a sense of newness and fresh insight.

Astronomy in Prehistoric Britain and Ireland, Clive Ruggles (Yale)

The Extraordinary Voyage of Pytheas the Greek, Barry Cunliffe (Penguin)

From Stonehenge to Modern Cosmology, Fred Hoyle (Freeman)

The Giddiness of Midsummer's Day, Dr Will Tosh (Shakespeare's Globe)

Handbook of Archaeoastronomy and Ethnoastronomy, Clive Ruggles (Yale)

Have a Cool Yule, Mélusine Draco (Moon Books)

Hearth & Garden: A Witch's Treasury, Gabrielle Sidonie (ignotus)

A Little History of Astro-Archaeology, John Mitchell (Thames & Hudson)

A Midsummer Night's Dream, William Shakespeare

The Modern Magical Revival: Esbats and Sabbats, Neville Drury (Brill)

Open Sandwiches: Smörgåsbord Ideas, Trine Hahnemann (Quadrille)

Scandinavian Comfort Food: Embracing the Art of Hygge, Trine Hahnemann (Quadrille)

Stonehenge Decoded, Gerald Hawkins (Hippocrene)

Stonehenge of the Kings, Patrick Crampton (Baker)

Welsh Folk Customs, Trefor M. Owen (Gomer Press)

The Wicker Man, Antony Shaffer and Robin Hardy (Hamlyn)

About the Author

Mélusine Draco is an Initiate of traditional British Old Craft and the Khemetic Mysteries. Her highly individualistic teaching methods and writing draw on historical sources supported by academic texts and current archaeological findings; endorsing Crowley's view that magic(k) is an amalgam of science and art, and that magic is the outer route to the inner Mysteries.

Author of several titles currently published with John Hunt Publishing including the best-selling six-part Traditional Witchcraft series; two titles on power animals – *Aubry's Dog* and *Black Horse, White Horse*; *By Spellbook & Candle; The Dictionary of Magic & Mystery* published by Moon Books; *Magic Crystals Sacred Stones* and *The Atum-Re Revival* published by Axis Mundi Books. Her esoteric novels, *House of Strange Gods* and *Realm of Shadow* are available in both paperback and e-book formats – all books are available on Amazon.

www.covenofthescales.com
www.templeofkhem.com
wordpress.com/view/melusine-draco.blog

MOON BOOKS BY MÉLUSINE DRACO

Traditional Witchcraft for...
Urban Living
The Seashore
Woods & Forests
The Pagan Revival
Fields & Hedgerows
The Path to the Mysteries

Pagan Portals
Have A Cool Yule
The (Inner-City) Path
By Spellbook and Candle
The Power of the Elements
Seeking the Primal Goddess
Pan: Dark Lord of the Forest
Sexual Dynamics in the Circle
By Wolfsbane & Mandrake Root
Divination: By Rod, Birds and Fingers
Sacred Landscape: Caves & Mountains

Other titles
The Atum-Re Revival
The Witch's Book of Simples
Magic Crystals, Sacred Stones
The Coarse Witchcraft Trilogy
The Dictionary of Magic & Mystery
The Aubrey's Dog: Canine Magical Lore
The Secret People: *Parish-pump witchcraft*
Black Horse, White Horse: Equine Magical Lore

MOON
BOOKS

PAGANISM & SHAMANISM

What is Paganism? A religion, a spirituality, an alternative
belief system, nature worship? You can find support for all these
definitions (and many more) in dictionaries, encyclopaedias, and
text books of religion, but subscribe to any one and the truth will
evade you. Above all Paganism is a creative pursuit, an encounter
with reality, an exploration of meaning and an expression of the
soul. Druids, Heathens, Wiccans and others, all contribute their
insights and literary riches to the Pagan tradition. Moon Books
invites you to begin or to deepen your own encounter, right here,
right now.

If you have enjoyed this book, why not tell other readers by
posting a review on your preferred book site.